genesis angels

By ARAM SAROYAN

GENESIS ANGELS
O MY GENERATION AND OTHER POEMS
THE STREET
POEMS
THE REST
CLOTH
WORDS & PHOTOGRAPHS
PAGES
ARAM SAROYAN

genesis angels

The Saga of Lew Welch and the Beat Generation

by

Aram Saroyan

WILLIAM MORROW AND COMPANY, INC.

NEW YORK 1979

Grateful acknowledgment is made for permission to use the following previously published material:

Epigraph by Jack Kerouac, from *On the Road,* Copyright © 1955, 1957 by Jack Kerouac. Reprinted by permission of Viking Penguin Inc.

Epigraph by Gary Snyder, from "North Beach" in *The Old Ways,* Copyright © 1977 by Gary Snyder. Reprinted by permission of City Lights Books.

"Further Notice," from *On Bear's Head,* Copyright © 1960, 1965, 1969 by Philip Whalen. (Harcourt Brace Jovanovich, Inc. and Coyote, New York.) Reprinted by permission of the author.

Excerpts from "Chicago Poem" and "Song of the Turkey Buzzard," from *Ring of Bone,* Copyright © 1973 by Donald Allen, Literary Executor of the Estate of Lew Welch. Reprinted by permission of Grey Fox Press.

Excerpts from correspondence by Lew Welch, Copyright © 1979 by Donald Allen, Literary Executor of the Estate of Lew Welch. Reprinted by permission of Grey Fox Press.

Library of Congress Cataloging in Publication Data

Saroyan, Aram.
Genesis angels: the saga of Lew Welch and the beat generation.

1. Welch, Lew—Friends and associates. 2. Authors, American—20th century—Biography. 3. Bohemianism—United States. I. Title. II. Title: Beat generation.
PS3573.E45Z87 811'.5'4 [B] 78-31172
ISBN 0-688-03436-5

BOOK DESIGN CARL WEISS

Printed in the United States of America.

First Edition

1 2 3 4 5 6 7 8 9 10

For My Mother

Special thanks to Donald Allen, Gary Snyder, Philip Whalen, Magda Cregg, Joanne Kyger, David Meltzer, Jack Hogan, Michael McClure, Bobbie Louise Hawkins, Michael Wolfe, Gregory Armstrong, Peter Warshall, Bill Deemer, Carol Matthau, Irving Lazar, Tim Yohn, Jason Hendrickson, John Brockman, Jim Landis, Norm Davis, Bill Berkson, and Gailyn Saroyan. And to the California Arts Council.

". . . and darkness was upon the face of the deep."

Genesis

"So in America when the sun goes down and I sit on the old broken-down river pier watching the long, long skies over New Jersey and sense all that raw land that rolls in one unbelievable huge bulge over to the West Coast, and all that road going, all the people dreaming in the immensity of it, and in Iowa I know by now the children must be crying in the land where they let the children cry, and tonight the stars'll be out, and don't you know that God is Pooh Bear? the evening star must be drooping and shedding her sparkler dims on the prairie, which is just before the coming of complete night that blesses the earth, darkens all rivers, cups the peaks and folds the final shore in, and nobody, nobody knows what's going to happen to anybody besides the forlorn rags of growing old, I think of Dean Moriarty, I even think of Old Dean Moriarty the father we never found, I think of Dean Moriarty."

—JACK KEROUAC,
On The Road

"In the spiritual and political loneliness of America of the fifties you'd hitch a thousand miles to meet a friend."

—GARY SNYDER

1

HE GREW UP IN A SUCCESSION OF LITTLE SOUND-ASLEEP California towns where the noise of children playing in the pastel light down the street is like butterflies of sound in the afternoon.

"Hey, Johnny!"

"Down *here*!"

And every so often a car goes by, slowly, to park in the driveway, slowly, three or four houses down. The tires taking their burden easefully up the little bump from the pavement to driveway, like a heavy sigh.

And boredom. Tricycles.

One kid down the street burning a bubble-gum comic with his magnifying glass, lying on his lawn one hand holding up his head, focusing the sun's rays to a little dot that makes a little yellow dot on the dumb comic, and then starts to smoulder.

His mother and his sister at home. A brilliant mother, absolutely no good to him; and then again, a fine and good lady. But no Dad.

His handsome father somewhere else, playing golf and sponging drinks, while Mom had the brains and the money. What kind of way is that for a boy to grow up in America with Tommy, Billy, Joey, Steve, Michael, and Stan.

Babe Ruth and Lou Gehrig.

John Garfield. Cagney and Bogart.

And they never lived anywhere more than three years anyway; so he was always the new guy in school.

In class. The guy that the most unpopular and strangely crippled personality—because determined nonetheless—maybe all kinds of kids are determined, just energetic—the one this goof, who may not even look particularly unusual, but is, because he collects envelopes instead of stamps, this is who comes up to Lew first of all the class and says:

"Hi, I'm Lester. What's your name?"

But Lew goes to so many different schools that he gets the hang of this critter he keeps magnetizing because he's new, that's all, and finally learns to be very cool, and wait for the *second* guy, who usually wasn't just a goof.

No, he was clearheaded: he had a wide, blue sky California type of mind. Howaryou. Well, wonderful. The kind of man Kerouac sometimes *looked* like, those open facial tones, but always retired to his room and marijuana and typewriter, out of the light, to think it over in typewritten home-movies of the old French-Canadian comic strip of all his friends and relatives. He was a real Proust through the American highway of Dreams.

Watching Neal and then, later, Lew himself drive the car. Because Kerouac didn't have that road savvy he loved in his heroes. Lew was as good as Neal he thought, too. A fine, extra smooth driver: just like his poems. Whereas Neal was Mr. Abyss, the guy who could take you right up to it: It!—and then swerve in time. Enlightenment through a sudden dispossession of self by way of the car.

Kerouac saw Lew as a hero too, but Lew was just as sophisticated as Jack, and that must have been hard to take. Lew was a red-headed, six-foot poet who knew all about Gertrude Stein, let alone Ezra Pound (he didn't even particularly *like* Pound, oh subterraneans), and knew how to tell exactly what he had in mind, elegantly.

Whereas Neal would Juggle words like a great Word Clown: and make you see new nouns and verbs peaking around corners of his sensibility, saying, "Hi, listen, you know I'm over here, too—I'll bet you thought I was just being myself, but I'm also the Universe! As are all men. And women. And kids. And this flower right here which I'm going to place in my lumberjack flannel shirt before I go to recap tires (my job) to pay for life and family (boy and girl) and my

Mrs. and subscriptions to *Popular Mechanics* and *Trained Parts* and *Art Today*, OK?"

Neal was a *driver*; Lew let the car do its job.

Clean appointments with turns: a joy of another order.

Nice sense of *time*.

Alcoholic, as opposed to the grass-head Neal Cassady, who could open up new cupboards in Space: here, Campbell's Soup. Want sandwiches?

Lew would tell you that everything was exactly what it seemed, even himself, although he had come from a ruined roaring twenties home, and was actually one-half F. Scott Fitzgerald unless he remembered to pay attention to everything. And be a normal, fine, happy, well-made man.

Handsome to women.

A man's man.

2

BECAUSE, DOWN DEEP AND AFTER ALL, HE KNEW HIS MOM did love him, and would light up his infant tantrums with her woebegone twenties flapper personality. Did she know how to handle a big infant boy, shitting and pissing, with a big dynamic Leo personality, bringing down the whole house if anything went wrong—who wanted his Mom's breast, and continuous smooth comfort, because there was American anxiety out the window, Great Depression casualties raining like cats and dogs out of the innocent, wide Western sky—and nobody with Big Papa hands to ease his entry into this dynamite country, full of aspirins and money schemes, and intelligent, neglected, then involuted women.

His Mom didn't know anything about children. She'd just fallen in love with Tyrone Power and Cary Grant combined in the person of "Speed" Welch from Kansas, who came on like a ton of bricks and made her relatively fine brains fall apart—big eye-contact dissolutions of all rhyme or reason, except the birds and bees floating down the Phoenix, Arizona, streets, into drugstores, and bar, big money parties with The Goldwaters: Lew reaches right into the real America, his nervous system could plunge right into the country club set—the chatter and splashes at the swimming pool; the attendant silently netting a leaf off the water's surface. And Lew was no fool.

The wind cut through the living room: the big American demon money buffaloed Speed Welch into cheating the very people got him placed in a distinguished banking job: responsibility among big denominations, new money, in neat, crisp, *heavy* wads. Yummo. And *his* Dad one of the nicest and finest lost-oes of all time, a judge back in Kansas. Because this man could not do anything properly but had a deep and fine moral personality, and anyway had lost all of the fingers on one hand in an accident on his farm. But he would be a fine judge, the community saw, and gave him that position out of love for his nature.

But Speed was sharp, and crooked—a fine athlete, with no money; and the pressure of the rich Brownfields, who got him all placed when their daughter fell in love with him, hopeless love, but what was there to do—because *her* Dad, the one Lew was the image of, Bob Brownfield, the guy with the brains, who would have seen through Speed Welch as if he were a window—because that was what he was, an American window—Bob Brownfield was dead.

And so Dorothy, his daughter, Lew's mother: her little son the very jewel of her father, born again (after a first miscarriage, also a boy, who Lew thought he was a reincarnation of too)—but what could she do with such a heavy, little rager beating on her little chest all of the time, because she didn't have enough milk for this colossus, Leo, infant boy, Lew Welch (his Dad Speed's real name, too), Jr.

And he didn't want to eat big ugly bowls of oatmeal. He wanted his disgraced and exiled father to put pressure on his demanding male, nervous system instead of driving the whole household wild every time he cried. He wanted big shoulder for his nap time, and then tuck him in—not Mom's boney shoulder, and lack of firm resolve on the tuck. Peaceful and quiet home with Pop there too.

And the poet got the taste of Death—the turning away from things, as he would turn away from the food; he lost interest then, at fourteen months: wouldn't eat, gave up, split, said fuck it, I give up, go ahead, bury me, you think I need this stupid world, fine, no more tantrums, forget the food, I don't need love, warm breast with plenty of milk, grace and light, the smell of mother, the smell of father—missing: and Lew wouldn't eat.

They put him in a hospital to get him fed. He had decided to let it go. Why suffer?

If his grandpa Bob had been around, the best surgeon in Phoenix, Lew wouldn't have been born in the first place to reincarnate that penetrating guy. Killed in a car crash in a car driven by Mrs. Goldwater, Barry's Mom, who loved the man and would have rather it be herself. A little tipsy from a party, she'd insisted on driving. Bob hadn't touched a drop because he had to do an operation that morning, but had let her have her way.

Lew had that ambivalent quality from infancy: he knew how to walk away. There was another side to this life, just around the corner of the mind, with more integrity to it. Deep peace and silence to put an end to the raging fires of his mind. Welch's intelligence went all the way to Death itself; the other side of it went all the way to the Earth Goddess, Mount Tamalpais, and the Turkey Buzzards silently circling.

And he loved women too, but with difficulty. His mother and his sister making the house a deep female prison at times, smothering his own, different growth. And yet . . . there was an intimacy in Welch's knowledge of his poor mother and sister that made his mind unusual, and exacting as a housekeeper's. Not a speck on the floor; everything in its place. Burning fever to get it all in place. Where's Dad?

And so Lew Welch entered the broken world of men, in baseball caps and denims, looking for the perfect play, because coming from a home with no father is as American as apple pie.

3

Because America began, was born inside of, the industrial revolution, and the myths of it involve this ability in man to transform himself into a precise instrument, even a machine, to accomplish a specific task that needed to be achieved, like whaling, harpooning Moby Dick, to light up the New England coast with lamps burning whale oil. So you get Ahab riding that whale, or is it his harpoon, into the watery grave of that great business enterprise, of which he was one of the Tycoons, whaling, his mind sharpened to a point.

And who knows what happened to his son, if he had one, unless he apprenticed himself to some local business, like making soap maybe, and learned the American ropes and ties and ladders that way. Because Dad in America from the outset is all confused with cash: and sometimes absent except in that disguise. George Washington, the Father of our country, on the dollar bill; Lincoln, who freed the Slaves and reversed that trend of business in making human prisoners (rounding 'em up easy by color separations), got the penny. Very funny.

Everybody gets to be a specialist. Precision parts makers of the great Dime Store of American Life. Hello, Ma'am. Why thank you, Sir. And men and women lose hold on the integrated domestic reality that gives each their lessons of the other—they may get married, and have families, but America divorces them into specialties like kitchens and children, and money and movement.

The traveling salesman and the milkman getting into all sorts of dirty jokes, because Dad's not home.

And by the time Jack and Neal and Lew get into it, F. Scott Fitzgerald is watching Jay Gatsby, who is the American man in the tradition of Ahab: a go-getter, all the way, but by now it's just money, and the mystery of it is the man himself: that huge American will and longing which has created the nation, and is now a little . . . wistful, maybe. And the woman is Daisy, the daughter of the money he created because he was born poor, and she is his obsession, and also his creation, the American rich girl, her voice "full of money." Is he still looking for cash? Fitzgerald only half the time, say.

While Hemingway took the great American will and focused it into sentences moving like precision parts in a machine that released—well, dread. He took big business American-made man into the green hills of Africa to hunt wild animals instead of cash, but the man was the same one. Or fishing the big two-hearted river. Because this man had been trained by the biggest machine of them all, War, which had created the perfect, self-destructing, product, so that the demand was endless: for bullets, bombs, or men.

And Lew and Jack and Neal were all gone within a few years of each other: shot out of the same American cannon, yet trying to turn into angels in mid-flight. *On the Road*, that saga of two lonely American-made men who dared to look into each other's eyes.

And that was Lew's loneliness, too. And he and Kerouac did share "a very sexy girl" in New York in 1959, and Lew loved Jack, but Lew was less driven. Like his driving style, compared to Neal's. Lew was more like the *next* generation, in a way, because his Mom had a Trust Fund, and he read boys' stories, and lived in Santa Monica, California, for a few years, way out West in the land of Dreams: motion picture starlets on the sidewalk. Footprints in the cement at Grauman's Chinese Theater. Popcorn, Mom, and Sis. And . . . Fred Astaire . . .

He had that relaxed attitude that could make a man of his generation an anomaly: a fuck-up like his grandpa Welch who could only handle moral refinements, finally. Disgrace? That ability to walk away; to drop the whole thing—from infancy. Life-death. And at the same time, balancing the world of men, his mother's quiet rooms. The emtpy bathroom all day.

Just switch on the light if you want to use it. Sensitive conversation.

Life-death and man-woman.

Whereas Kerouac was a different physical type entirely. And wrote a twelve-hundred-page novel, and then got his style (which he couldn't get published for seven years nevertheless). He opened himself wide with different drugs, lighting himself up and knocking himself off, a pinball wizard, balancing chemistries for the right prose mix. And he took the tip from Neal's conversation—cause Neal was an amateur writer, but a *professional* American—to get it all in.

When you get to the end of the sentence, don't stop, because there are secrets waiting to be born of your own generosity, if you will be sincere, and honest, and open-hearted. Hearts.

American hearts. And minds. But you can do a new kind of thing with the heart. Look at great Allen Ginsberg. Made it to the West Coast and let out *Howl*, that roller-coaster mantra that cracked the iron grip of the fifties; and wrote it like Jack wrote prose, transposed his style into poetry. Why?

Because Allen loved Neal too, and wouldn't take no for an answer, and Neal loved Allen's incredible and important determination to be whole, and love, himself.

These were the shock troops, the very pioneers of love in America: and they had to love each other first, before and more importantly than women, because their Dads had all gotten cashed in for chips. Or caved in completely.

Neal's an old Denver flophouse wino.

Jack's a printer: so his son loved printing his own little grade school newspaper. And real stories of his mind: Kerouac got to *employ* his Dad, in the end (not literally), by being a writer.

Lew's Dad taught him how to fish.

4

BECAUSE "SPEED" WELCH WOULD SHOW UP AGAIN EVERY NOW and then and the household would click into new, yet ancient ratios—rekindling that old Douglas Fairbanks-Mary Pickford chemistry that had rocked the Phoenix class structure, and made Speed shakey and criminal in his pursuit of balanced identity amidst the rich and smart. Still a very handsome presence, this man, and Dorothy took to him all over again once, twice, three times, through the years, though never for long enough for Lew to get in any more than a zap of fish-hunt, with my Dad. Dropping a line here off Santa Monica pier; giving a .22 a try in a field with a couple of tin cans.

Discovered right away: the boy had an eagle-eye, a vulture's, a Turkey Buzzard's far-sighted precision. He had a way with the gun, which his Pop handed him a couple of times, along with the fishing rod, and his own grown-man's dark brown smell. A moment or two in the undivided light of his father's nature. Enough to give him these gifts, which he held onto through the years. His own father's skills and triumphs: his own birthright.

And also discovered through the coach that he could sprint faster than anyone in school in the sixth grade, even though Dorothy had been convinced by some off-the-wall American salesman to fit the boy with steel-trap shoes, which atrophied his arches. Too much support crippling the same as too little.

"Pop!"

"Hello, Lewie!"

He took off the steel-traps, ran barefoot, and beat everybody, just a little guy then, and very fast, like his Dad had been in college football and gotten dubbed "Speed."

The speed and the precision from Lew to Lew, Jr. And the natural world, too. Taking the rod and reel to Malibu and casting into the surf for perch. The world that is not man that the father, fleetingly, showed his boy. And the boy remembered forever.

And the Mom, Dorothy, read him stories and showed him how to use the pleasant, local California library, dust motes floating in the sunlight, punctuated by the small shoe-noises, and whispers: the Church of Knowledge, the Hospital of the Soul. The print in all kinds of fine texts, free.

And in the seventh grade, a man named Robert Rideout, tells his class that if you like a book, you'll probably like another book by the same writer. Clean intelligence. Not just information. And Lew read a hundred and sixty books that year from *Lassie* to *Mutiny on the Bounty*. A teacher. A coach. Anybody that Lew could look to who might give him what was missing.

And his Mom read Virginia and him stories every night: she was a fine woman in her own ways.

And that same year, seventh grade, Rideout showed them poetry:

> Poems are made by fools like me.
> But only God can make a tree

And his heart was there right away, out in the West of America, being given the goods by the community in the best way it could manage for its native sons and daughters. The place makes itself up inside each one, telling itself over and over. And California is *mild*.

A balm to the heart and the mind.

A palm tree on the sidewalk. Third- and fourth-graders walking around with important poems born inside their quizzical minds; sixth-graders like Lew really serious about being alive, and running, and reading, and going to movies, and a very beautiful girl (pure spirit in a dazzling complexion) two seats away, studying.

Lunchtime Tom has a firecracker; saving it for after school, because here comes Mr. Louis.

"Hello, boys."

"Hi, sir."

And you can feel words in this atmosphere, spread out under the sky, stucco Spanish-style low-set buildings, and ice-cream shops and colors: you can feel words, one at a time, going by in native American combinations: slower, with a slow savor like a lick off a peach ice-cream cone, a slow lick, than you can feel them, say, in the middle of New York City (going on at the same time, across the country: as well as Paris, Istanbul, and Uganda—worlds).

You can hear a word like "flower" in California, and it seems like a beautiful invention of the air, just like the flower itself.

Lew got that kind of modern mind in the wide open spaces of those California towns: hushed, with a swimming pool in the back and no one there but a dog, asleep, on the diving board. And inside, Jimmy's Mom makes root beer floats. Unbelievable flavor.

In a way, the perfect background to become an advertising man: the word made real in the soft light of suburban California.

His feet had gotten goofed-up bad though with those steel-traps (Mom coming on too strong) and he needed tennis shoes instead and his coach backed him up at home (Dad replaced). He won. The balance struck, but the damage was real.

Lew Welch walked backward for the entire year he spent in the ninth grade. He wouldn't take another crutch, and he couldn't walk normally. So you have the poet going inside to get outside, and outside to get inside: a deep intelligence necessary, to keep on walking, and keep on talking.

5

WHEREAS JACK AND NEAL ARE SIMULTANEOUSLY BEING shaped, being rhythmically determined, you might say, by the music of entirely different American states (the United States would come later when they all unlocked their natures to one another, and created that mystical-chemical compound known as the Beat Generation, discovered by *Time* and *Life*, which released new and liberating vibrations all over). Jack in Lowell, Massachusetts, which is New England: a factory town, with men going to work in gray eight in the morning cold, carrying lunch in brown paper bags. And Neal in Denver, in the middle of America, the real orphan of them all: a mother not even in the picture, and a father lost in an old stiffened overcoat, with old newspapers rolled in the pockets, and no eyes. A terrible shrouded stranger, an American statistic, the zero man.

And Neal, somehow, finding the light in this guy, his Dad, following him around, a youngster walking in and out of the flophouse glooms and dooms: guys staring through forty-five-year-old erosions of their psyches: Neal was the one who had visited the suites and pavilions of absolute nowhere, he of them all knew the American basement, the bottom, the elevator busted . . . It's all over. He had that knowledge to touch the others with, if they could see through his glamour, because Neal of all of them was the movie star: a mythic man who burned energy that was made up of circuits grabbed out of the American air itself: like a juggler grabs a plate, a cup, a saucer, and a spoon, say, and throws them up into motion, creating a new, mobile constellation in front of everybody of these normally ordinary items.

So Neal would steal: a car, a waitress, a ride into the hills, a sexual treat, the moonlight, danger, lost conversational pyramids, sudden mythic Union, the mind's own onion. This is the man who invented the spontaneous bop prosody that Jack, being sophisticated (a sophisticated artist tuning into his generation), copied down like Boswell: because it was Neal, whom he loved the way he loved his Dad, actually, the big fat guy printer who knocked a rabbi off his feet by bopping out his stomach at the Jew (in the deep French-Canadian inbred, smothering hate and confusion and paranoia of a gloomy minority)—Kerouac saw all his father's vain hopes and energetic disappointments (before fat and negativity, before tragedy and anti-semitism rented him entire) in flashing, gnashing, dashing Neal. The American Dream.

And so Neal, as Kerouac's Dean Moriarty in *On the Road*, and in his own angelic availability (like a movie star's in fact: "I'll take the call! If they want me at the premiere in Pocatello, I'd better go." A show business hustler's savvy), became a kind of American mental male Pin-Up, out in crazy diners at four in the morning, having straight-ahead conversations with the waitress and the young truck driver, talking wide-open in the mysterious American night, with big cargoes hurtling by in the deep star-studded highway night: chilly outside. Betty Grable in the movies and dreams, the woman like a delicious and ripe fact of our universe; and Neal Cassady with his own come-hither look at this whole generation of pioneering artists: "Come on over here, boys, it's me: America, a strong man with love inside." Kerouac saw the broken dream of his father—now a gloomy printer, resentful—and maybe his own self, riddled in Neal's American mirror.

Because the guy had no past, and no future, just like the American Dream, just like the industrial giant: King-Kong with an airplane crashing off his wrist, is America. The nervous system all out of proportion to the actual human world, the natural world being ravaged by it. King-Kong up there on the top of the Empire State Building with Fay Wray in his arms and the airplane bothering him: that is a portrait, in its way, of our American-made mind, a colossus, a gorilla, but underneath, human. The infant inside the towering monster: you and me.

This was some situation comedy everybody was in, and it had to move West to get a little distance, a little space, a little perspective on itself. And out West was Lew, who was a likewise handsome American man, taller, with a different set of sensibilities, but eager and gregarious as the rest. An ex-Chicago advertising copywriter by now, glad the boys had done this big thing in American writing, because it had gotten him back into real life, after Chicago crack-up and psychoanalysis. Lew is, physically, unstable. Jack and Neal are smaller, heavier men: more solid.

And Lew is a poet, which means that at a certain point, no matter how magnetic the gallery of players, and pints, and quarts, and gallons, this man has this double, life-death nature deep inside him: the stillness of the undifferentiated life-form, the cosmic stone, unspeaking, void: the nothing that is in fact everything, birds, trees, Mom, Dad, and is in fact Lew. And he saw it from both sides. He was a poor and fine poet, who really couldn't be employed, who could take a year on something that couldn't get him a dime, because he wasn't going for stories, for novels, for anything, really: which is the deep dilemma of the poet. He was going for nothing. That was what was inside him.

Nothing that is cups, and sunlight, trolley cars and bread. Old California history books deep in brown sunlight. A poet is like light: pure information. The colors occur according to what's placed in front of it, light.

Lew was light, and then Lew again. He loved Jack (and Neal, practically the same man) but he was already on to another kind of mind, he was half himself sometimes to be finally one. He wanted the whole thing, including everybody, and the wheeling planet. And it was all there, perfectly, if he could be there.

And sometimes he could.

6

In high school, now in Palo Alto, in Northern California after starting in the Southwest, that heat and space, and graduating gradually into the cooler regions of milder, coastal geographies—now Lew is a track star, a pool hustler, and making his first poems out of the air in his mind.

And he's having the difficulty common to the poet, beginning with a feeling for the words, and the way they move: the yellow, green, blues, reds, oranges, and browns—the deep purple moods they could conjure through themselves, moving along on a current in the mind's eye.

They can take over: and build buildings, and create caves, and investigate crimes, and take the mind with them right out of the San Francisco Bay Area, and into a new moonlit nowhere of the mind that has no relation to anywhere.

And Lew would stop here, and wonder.

Hey, words, where you going? Where you taking me? Today I walked Susan home, and we talked about the chemistry exam (and Jim went by on his bicycle) and her Mom, Helen, was watering their lawn when we got there around 4:30, overcast. And this is not what the words are about. I'm an American in the air on the land among the buildings and personalities and I want to tell what happens, truthfully.

Lew being a Leo, full of fire, a personality, winning, a runner, and the words would catch this personal energy and ride it into their own worlds, leaving Lew to be honest, because being a poet really has very little to do with "having a good imagination" as they say in school. Being a poet has to do with giving up those poses, and slants, and persuasions, and tractions, and liabilities, and assurances that words and the mind are prone to—and being there.

Being here, very simple, very quiet, with almost nothing at all in mind, in fact nothing at all: which is so full and deep that it is day and night, midnight and noon, as the poet is this world, himself, always.

The poem is the real.

And it is born in the mind that, momentarily, abandons its positions, defenses, and patterns of being, and simply is—as, suddenly, momentarily, everything around it, is.

Lew's mind was still getting its bearings in its medium, and the language was holding sway, and he would start to write and the metaphor would get so big, he couldn't see what was in front of him anymore; the words took over, and gave him deep sea grottoes, celestial architecture, vast columns of perishing empires of the air: all bad poetry, he knew, by the instinct that was and is the poet's deepest nature.

Equanimity.

The place in the nature of a person in which all things are simply themselves, simultaneously, as that person is, among them.

Being one of them.

And just being.

And the problem of the poet in America or the poet anywhere in the world is the problem of anyone anywhere: how to do this, because it is the deepest and most beautiful knowledge of the world, oneself, matter, time, energy, reality, universe, telephone, and giraffe. It is everything.

Because each is itself.

The pencil is exactly the pencil.

Perfect.

The mirror is empty, and full.

And the sound of one hand clapping is the sound of two hands clapping because that is the sound of one hand clapping.

Lovemaking.

That ability and inclination to let ourselves be what we are. No more and no less

Than what we are, openly, in the world.

And everything is what it seems.

This is timeless, and dangerous, and worthy of our love and devotion.

When the mind empties, the Hindus say, the heart fills it—and that is poetry, that simple time.

So you have this young guy trying to get the words to stop getting carried away by his terrific, imaginative, Leo, powerful personality: the runner, and pool shark (precision, timing—"Eight ball in the corner pocket . . ."), and red-headed handsome young man. Because the words open truly in the poet when all that is still: the words come by then, singly, or in phrases, in swirls and eddies, made up of the real air of the real breezes in Palo Alto in the mid-forties, when you have Lew just himself, practically nothing at all.

And this isn't America, or Japan, India or Africa.

It's nothing: where everything is, immediately.

And to have a young man getting in training, and trying to get through the complications, and the whole rigamarole of education, and identity, and society, and sex, and success, and masculinity, and femininity, and radio ("The Shadow knows . . . Heh heh heh . . . "), and Uncle Sam Wants You (because Lew was going there too)—this is the great comedy and tragedy of our exact lives, now as well as then. Lew was a poet.

And he was incisive.

A strong, analytical, dry, sharp mind to try to cut through the interruptions of his time and place in civilization. To get through, to cut through—to what is. That flower right there every second.

America was training another poet.

And he was running: the 440 in 49.8, once.

Lew Welch was fast and smart—and a poet. He wanted the words to be in place, precisely themselves for the poem, when it happened to him. And that is making it happen, too.

7

Young John Kerouac, on the other side of the country, has been awarded a football scholarship to Columbia University in New York City up on 116th Street, where Harlem and Lionel Trilling intersect, in an extraordinary urban mambo step—and this deeply parochial, yet also suddenly and comically complete and open personality, Kerouac, is going to go to Horace Mann Prep School in Morningside Heights to get him properly acculturated for the step into the hallowed halls of C. And here is John, who has already filled nickel notebooks with important stories influenced by Hemingway, and Saroyan, and Thomas Wolfe—nickel notebooks full of woe and glee—and had an enormous personal victory, scoring a high school touchdown that got the Columbia coach to pay heed, and money.

Out of the French-Canadian haunted, New England smoke and factory doomed streets of Lowell, this good but only half-known (to himself) young writer and football player, is suddenly right here in the Big Apple—42nd Street at night, the Empire State Building, one man standing on the corner beside a huge building containing hundreds of lives going on in apartments. TV has been born. People are inside their rooms watching Milton Berle, and Sid Caesar and Imogene Coca. The war is on, but Kerouac won't last long in the Navy—honorably discharged for an "indifferent character." He's not a good soldier and he's not even much of a football player, according to coach Lew Little who so pisses off Kerouac's Dad by not letting his son off the bench.

John—*Jack's* getting disillusioned by sports. His father comes to talk to the coach, even. There's some influence, maybe cosmic, turning Kerouac out of his football plays and over onto the page, where he would later make passes and catches and big never-to-be-repeated touchdowns into green ebullience and radiant earth blues. Oh, October on the steps of the dream.

And one night—in the history of you and me—at the West End Bar, with alive tables and chairs and beers, and incredible conversations about everything under the sun, under the electric light—with West Side traffic outside, and goofed-up drunks, and young couples, husband with his tie loosened, wife with a new permanent—one night John Kerouac is introduced across the table to young, deep-fabled, not long out of New Jersey, Allen Ginsberg.

This is the primal meeting, the plug-in that reverses historical currents and lights up new rooms in the mind of generations. One poet and another poet, in America, getting to know the drift of their own, single mind: Hello, I see you. Hello, I see you, too.

And it's John who really has to make the jump, and become Jack. Allen is already Allen in New York, or at least more familiar, although being gay is another dimension of himself, nagging at his attention—for complete disclosure, not quite yet. And here's John: Mr. America (and Allen must dream of these heroes).

But what you really have is the two ends of the spectrum of the American man, both with enormous reserves of energy and intelligence, clicking together, instantly, because they're both poets, and you have instantly one of the rarest facts of this time (and ours): friendship. Which is the electric hookup of human energy that doubles the pleasure, doubles the fun, and makes everybody feel swell.

This did not happen between Hemingway and Fitzgerald, no. They have told a different story, already.

This is what happened between Ginsberg and Kerouac—not even Mailer and Baldwin—and what released, in others, equal friendship, and started the cosmic cross-country dance that went on as Rock and Roll was being born (Chuck Berry and Little Richard on the sound track on the radio), and everybody in the midst of the Quietest decade yet, started getting goofed-up and happy, and making a new kind of bright red literary art.

Now listen to me.

It's these two guys not standing on custom, habit, tradition, or even pride, or humility, or anything else, but saying OK, Ginsberg, you be Allen, and OK, Kerouac, you be Jack —that old I'm OK You're OK they're writing books about twenty years later, like it's just coming to be, best sellers—hahaha. This is the music that can steal us all faster than you can say Tutti Frutti gonna rutti bob bop a loo la a dom dom dang. This is the first condition of music, you might say.

Allen and Jack, breaking through French-Canadian spook and Jewish torment, the nuclear moment, the blast, of friendship and love.

And if there is anything at all that makes the Beat Generation more than a bunch of interesting and beautiful creations of words recording collections of deeds, it's this beautiful moment (and lifetime) of friendship that fired it, and squired it, and wired it, and made it a gyre, fanning waves of communion through the planet news. You've got to give Allen and Jack credit for the ability to be friends, literary friends, and close personal portrait painters of one another—and it just goes to prove what that particular human development can do.

Everybody getting honest because friendship allows you: honesty, sincerity—and getting funny, naked, real and red: because affection will let it. Rhythm, and health, and humor, and new ideals in art: instead of the New Criticism of maze-in-maze on John Donne: John Donne's simple honest speech, his ax of love.

Friendship released new ingredients in the recipes of art, and one by one began a new community across all the lines.

8

AND THE YOUNG POET, LEW WELCH, WHO DOESN'T KNOW HE'S a poet yet, who thinks he may be a musician or a painter—his mind is an inventor's mind, in fact, like Bob Brownfield's mind, who figured out how to "pull" tonsils and also wrote short stories back in Phoenix—and the next step in life's agenda, underwritten by the universe, co-signed by God, and sponsored without ceremony by the nation, was to be called up by the United States Army Air Corps (where he'd signed up at seventeen) and sent to—lo!—Denver where he spent most of his service time (1944-45) in training, before being released at the end of the war. No combat. No contest.

Lew is such a good shot he substitutes for his buddies on the rifle range to get them high ratings in marksmanship.

He takes piano lessons (having earlier tried clarinet).

He probably walks right by rushing, and by now locally legendary Neal Cassady (on his way to some appointment with the gas-pedal to the stars): his engine already careening through lives and loves, as fast as a speeding bullet, powerful as a locomotive, locked in the Midwest, ready to go discover every kind of conversation, new ideas in each American: ready to go! Neal was Ahab too, and Jay Gatsby, but the game had changed: he saw his heart locked in the American super-highway, the four-lane black-top: topped by the stars. He was reeling to get real, unraveling all the red tape of desperate, post-adolescent mania to get placed, and nothing but the gas station for home and a job.

He was stealing cars for joy-rides; stealing virgins and waitresses from the town fathers and local commerce. He was hungry for the culture that hadn't been born; starving for his own name and date with America. Lew probably passed him out there, and wondered to himself: "Hmm, that guy needs something: this is the Midwest, Colorado (beautiful word, you could make a song out of), lock a melody on that one and it would be all over, get Sinatra or Billy Eckstein to give it resonance. You know I could be a singer, too, maybe I should sing it. That guy was *racing*, yeah, he had his own *beat*."

A young soldier thinking and walking along the Denver sidewalk in his uniform, passing jewelry stores (real diamonds, tiny ones, for sale) and luncheonettes, where beautiful and not-so-beautiful native Denver American women are out serving and entertaining with their smiles and personalities. The sun is shining and he walks on to look at the stills outside the movie theater.

Or comes out of it in daylight with his buddy, just a few people during the afternoon scattered through the plush upholstery and baroque decor, and coming out he's got to give his eyes a chance to adjust to the daylight. Because it was night inside the theater, and a big dream on the screen, *To Have and Have Not* (not bad).

Lew was an American musician, letting the sounds ripple through him, to play them back with a steadier attention later, in his poems. Archibald MacLeish said a poem must not mean, but be. And that was the melody, for Lew. He had that California ear where you hear the words on the air, unfolding with rare clarity for America—words like "sure," and "favor," making soft landings on the ear.

And he did have the ability to sing like Billy Eckstein. With red hair.

And one day, the old man, "Speed" Welch shows up at the base, and father and son greet and see each other, and look away and look back, for the last time, as the planet turns, Speed gone at forty-seven. Here he is, the handsome old devil, gone soft and hollow cheeked with American failure: deep misunderstanding between him and the nation, between him and Dorothy, and now look at his boy: tall fellow, taller than him. After all, just an American, happy athlete, Speed had been: high spirits, love for nature, a Kansas man, how did it get so god awful complicated?

And Lew sees and knows his father out of the circuits of his mother's home, sees the chiseled fact of time the man is, with his mistakes and earthly erasures, his pride and defeat, the song of the wind inside him, the wild handsome style that did not quite fit the American world (as Neal's style neither, quite fit; as Lew's own, wouldn't)—because the nation is there, but unborn. Men walk around in dreams of themselves; women walk in their own. The movies are there; the television is melting away the local styles and country ways: but the people are coming and going just the same.

Lew got a good strong look into his lifelong absent father's face before it faced back into itself, and was gone. The glamour and madness of his father's decade, the twenties, all done and forgotten. F. Scott Fitzgerald trying to get Irving Thalberg to give him a good shot at a screenplay; and then making him the model for a sudden, last, clear take on the model of Gatsby: a movie mogul.

But what is failure, and what is success. What is the principle involved? The boy had grown; the father had aged—and the two said hello and good-bye for the first and last times under the flat American sky, each as grown men. Lew had a good eye with the rifle, which his father had first handed to him.

It's time that makes the emotion, a law of its nature is the unfolding of feeling. But America was still too young for time: a child that doesn't know it will ever be gone from the green, impervious earth. And Lew was a young man, still too young to know that fact of mortality that comes in the middle of life, when the distance between the present and death is less, and we are most ourselves, the energy of our actual lives.

It was Speed Welch who knew it, seeing his red-headed, open-eyed son in his uniform.

9

AND IN NEW YORK, ALLEN GINSBERG IS LYING ON A COUCH in some forgotten East Harlem apartment—with sunlight real on the red brick escarpment he sees through the window, other windows, unknown lives—a young man, lost in Manhattan's neon wilderness, and in the neural wilderness of his own impulses: young, and full of energy, which, like Neal Cassady's, strains against the limits of his time and civilization (subway gum machine mirrors, hello soul of Allen). And he is writing exact transcriptions of his mind and heart's stasis—the lack of flow registered in bad dreams, and unhappy times. Jinxed by time, a poet in a gone age—lying on a sofa in the afternoon.

But Allen is careful. Allen won't jump; he has the semitic skepticism the others would need and value in him later. He is, despite a marijuana thought here and there, the rarest of young poets of this age in his singular gift of—sobriety. Allen will wait out the blues, let the jukebox shift in heaven: his own 45 will turn up on the turntable one of these days. This man, deep in his own abyss, loves himself: the breath and hair, cock and balls, eyes and back and ass, he is struck with his own sullen, perhaps, but nevertheless given, completeness. And he will, least of all of his friends, do violence to the God-given form he is. Allen Ginsberg loves himself, and the self he sees echoing through the others: and he is the binding agency of the unit, the force of his love is the centering it all needs. That he sees, and breathes, and does no harm.

Younger than Kerouac: but a Jew, ancient in his own fable, and wise in the unspoken knowledge of time's style. He may rush, at times; but he feels the distance in himself—not out there. When will I let you love, Allen; when will you be the real Allen. And he is patient, and kind, and keeps his body fed, and doesn't go down drug's drain.

Allen has a mother and a father. His mother, Naomi, driven mad by American Socialist Workers nightmares and dis-ease; his father, Louis, a poet and school teacher of Paterson, New Jersey. He is, in this sense, literally and in the cohesion of his home, and relatives, aunts and uncles, his brother who has a good job and a wife, a *second* generation. Hence, the sense of time absent among others born and unborn on the American Now: the instant improvising and perishing away, always (Neal—sometimes Jack too).

Even being gay, in the late forties when almost no one would speak of it openly, cannot unhinge the basic sanity Allen Ginsberg is. And then, lying there on the sofa, waking and sleeping at the same time in the afternoon of unemployed Manhattan thought-dream identity fixes, suddenly Allen hears the voice of the poet in the book he's got out and looks into.

"Ah, sunflower, weary of time . . . "

He hears William Blake, the angel, the real Blake, in the voice of his own words, giving him the message of his poem in a later century in another, denser, city: the honks of traffic below, the miscellaneous street crashes and yelps occurring in present time: he hears the eternal voice of Blake breaking through the brain's stubborn contours of today, and me, and you. And his heart swells with vision and the blessing of this seer—who sees through time to him. Allen Ginsberg in Manhattan. Allen Ginsberg with a late afternoon guest, William Blake, unlocked out of a book.

Saying hello from heaven inside the very room: ah, breezes. Thank you, room. Thank you, light. Thank you, red brick outside. Thank you, sidewalk circumstances and incidental noises. Thank you, wall. Thank you, bookprint which held this voice for me, focusing it on the phrases created in another century.

In England, great Blake. Thank you, too, Allen, for being calm for so clear a revelation, being available in New York City, of all places, for the Vision—the voice, in the afternoon light. Allen who loves himself as Blake loves himself as Shakespeare loves Hamlet and the world as Emily Brontë and

Dickinson love their own bibles of unfolding selves: as all the immortal world loves. Allen says thank you for his own, steady, grace.

The poet's heart has filled his mind again, and the heart's voice was Blake: cutting through the mazes of the civilized afternoon, and Time.

Wait till Kerouac hears about this.

And Jack hears, and takes it with big (gulping) smiles of religious curiosity (Jack a born Catholic) and just the right amount of football player leer, to let Allen know he's Jack after all, part of their deal from the beginning. Nobody disintegrates; everybody reintegrates.

"Aw, Allen, let's get sandwiches at the West End, you foolish poet Jew. Did I ever tell you about my father and the rabbi. I don't know if I can trust you to understand. My father is—was—tragic, Allen. Can you understand this?"

The currents are strengthening.

"Hey, and maybe we should give that queer Burroughs a call. Jesus, what a weirdo!"

"Do you want to hear the story of my father and the rabbi —Ginsberg! Answer me, Mr. Blake!"

Because Kerouac's father has died in 1946 in Jack's arms, and his tragedy and legacy is the writer's original and enduring work. Kerouac is now out of Columbia, as is Allen—both school problem cases—and Jack is writing his first book, his twelve-hundred-page *The Town and the City*, about Lowell and New York, and everything, the football game, Lew Little, his proud father (idealized): it's a book like Thomas Wolfe wrote. He's got huge sentences inside him.

10

Lew Welch, studying English and music now at College of the Pacific and Stockton Junior College, back in the pastel light and air of Northern California, getting together his internal orchestra; he wants to play melodies, or paint them or say them, and he's running at Stockton on a $600 a year track scholarship, and being a fraternity brother, and having trouble consummating his relationships—he can't get laid, nobody would do it. This is the late forties, and Lew is a regular guy among guys and girl friends. Oh, America, coming around the bend of a new decade, all dressed up in new postwar (cold-war) commodities and possibilities. Young couples getting married to make a home for major appliances . . . Samsonite luggage . . . Bendix freezers . . .

And Lew Welch, our California poet—poet-laureate of Mount Tamalpais later in the history of Marin County—is trying to decide what he should do with his simple, red-headed, intelligent life. Maybe I should be a big restaurant owner for the stars, and smoke big cigars? . . . Maybe I should drink a beer and make a painting of the sky with just a few trees . . . I am me, and my knees; my mind is keen, my pen is out of ink, I believe. And there is this teacher, James Wilson, the kind of man who opens the classroom out into an experience of knowledge and intelligence and affection: an artist teaching . . . and he has made an impression on Lew, who has that lingering space, that absence where his father wasn't there, and is open to a strong presence he can feel is real. Because Lew is discriminating, keenly discerning among people: he never really falls for people out of desperate need, but makes judgments and seeks out what he sees can feed his own need.

He is unusually intelligent.

Instinctively correct.

He goes into James Wilson's office one afternoon with the intention of speaking to him about something. He is not sure what he wants to speak to him about, but he is coming to some kind of reckoning. He feels an urgency. And Jim Wilson is not there. The room is empty.

But the room is full of Jim Wilson, anyway: his papers and his books strewn across his desk. The presence of the man permeates the atmosphere, and Lew sits down and decides to wait until Jim Wilson returns, no matter how long it takes. He decides to make himself at home in this man's absent presence, as all his life he has known his father's present absence: and in fact the two are almost indistinguishable. He sits down in his father's house, and no one is aware he is there. And he is saved.

It happens like this.

He picks up a copy of *Three Lives* by Gertrude Stein off Jim Wilson's desk (out the window, a big campus tree, birds, students strolling out of view) and he reads the long story "Melanctha" and he becomes a writer.

Everybody has been telling him that Gertrude Stein is "a rose is a rose is a rose"; but when he reads this story in Gertrude Stein's first book he sees that Gertrude Stein is not a rose is a rose is a rose, or not just so, because Gertrude Stein is putting her words together so clearly and simply in this story of a young black woman and her suitor that there is no way for Lew Welch not to understand what it is that writing really is. And he becomes a writer. He reads Gertrude Stein and sees what writing is and he becomes a writer.

Writing is putting words together one after another in such a way that there is no mistaking that it is writing and yet at the same time there is no mistaking that it is the truth. And this is what Gertrude Stein is doing, so simply and forcefully and carefully, in her story about Melanctha and her suitor. Lew cannot mistake it.

It is clear.

And he is clear.

And it is writing that has made him clear.

And Jim Wilson isn't there—still hasn't arrived.

But in the meantime Lew has had the vision.

Gertrude Stein has arrived inside him to make writing clear and simple and a good thing for someone to do, and so Lew is a writer.

He knows that now: he is clearly a writer, because he sees so clearly what it is to be a writer.

He has been a sports reporter for the paper, but he didn't know then. And he has been writing since high school but it still wasn't clear until he read this story in the room of a man who had gotten his attention, and filled a space in his life, that needed something, and then gone to this man but found him not in: found him not in, but nevertheless there, and settled himself in a chair in the midst of this man's presence, and picked up a book from this man's desk, and read a long story, and been given his life's work.

Because the story was so clear. And he became so clear reading it.

Like Allen Ginsberg hearing Blake's voice in a lonely Manhattan afternoon, and knowing the love in the creator, Lew Welch has experienced the clarity and love and purpose and simplicity of the creator in the writing of Gertrude Stein's "Melanctha."

And he has found his life—it has cut through to him through Stein.

And later he talks to Jim Wilson about it, and Wilson nods and smiles, and suggests that maybe Lew ought to try a place called Reed College up in Oregon, that might be a good place for a writer to go.

And that's where Lew goes.

11

WILLIAM SEWARD BURROUGHS, SCION OF THE ADDING MAchine fortune (founded by his grandfather), was precise and impassive in his exploration of the underside of the American Dream, and drama.

A small trust fund enabling him to remain unemployed, a Harvard graduate interested in writing, he gravitated to the underworld characters and haunts, picking up the jargon and the various cons in various Eighth Avenue bars off of Times Square where men discussed the sale or theft of, for instance, a machine gun.

Burroughs carried another world inside him: the affluent, St. Louis childhood, combined with the sense of his own difference, his own separation from his given life and parents and education: he was immaculate in personal habit, and mental pattern. He saw what he saw without remarks.

A tall, gray visage, in a business suit, with vest, and an interest in hallucinogens. But not a great European saint of the underworld like Genet, or a great emotional expositor of liberation like crackers Artaud—Artaud was crackers. Burroughs was like a zen monk of guns, drugs, saps, and cons: the whole carny world of freaks and fallouts, odd shots, and dropouts, queers and junkies, in which he finally felt, simply, at home.

Bill Burroughs had a mask of cool, immovable indestructible cool, and since people really are what they pretend to be, so Bill Burroughs was, in fact, that very thing—plus he had a wicked sense of humor that would scare and delight Jack and Allen when they visited him downtown in his Village apartment. A nut case.

Masquerading as an American decadent, yet in fact a part of the new neural intelligence of the Beat Generation: the little discoveries possible in the writing when there is no attitude worth espousing, nothing to see but what is there:

A chorus of tiny men doing a Radio City Music Hall number across the bed-covers at four in the morning, snowing.

A voice—a demon—discovered in the water faucet, saying why-you-fool-ha-ha-ha-why-you-fool-hahaha, saying demonized gibberish, and also discovered in the noise of traffic outside, and in eventually all noise until a man is being mocked by everything in the universe that has a noise: and that is HIS noise, his mantra speaking to him.

"Why hello, Allen, dear. And Jack. How lovely of you to come. Sit down. Sit down. Would you like a cup of tea with turbinado sugar."

"I'll take the tea, OK, Burroughs, but I don't want any turpentine."

"Now, Jack. Let's not get paranoid. I was offering you health food."

"OK, Bill. I'll bite. Hahaha haraaa."

In America, each of us is a stranger. The communities are mostly too large. Our neighbors are sphinxes, as we are to them. Passionate men and women are confused and rendered inefficient, and suspicious of their own enthusiasm and energy. We hide the poem written in our own soul, or offer it obliquely to the light: daisies in the city window, roses on the dining car table: the landscape speeds by, and our dream is unloosed in meaningless efforts: buying and selling pieces of a lost vocabulary of feeling, the dollars and cents can never replace.

These Beat people were gardening in each other's real earth, starting to water and plant a new estate of the mind in the midst of American urban commerce. All the rehearsals of their identities are now like sacred texts of the genesis of an original, native American culture. We hunger for more of the truth of ourselves which they allowed themselves to be.

Nobody was so poor anymore, so people (and artists with sharp eyes) began to investigate important states of being, instead of just stating the case over and over again, rendering it meaningless in repetition.

Crazy is as crazy does; likewise sanity; likewise a man.

Allen and Jack and Bill dropped the "idea" for the real thing, say, a human being. What is it like to be a human being at three in the morning in New York City in the history of the universe, 1949, Bickfords Cafeteria 14th Street.

Their text scribbled on available napkins and teletype rolls, driving no point home. Driving nothing, but their own human, circulating blood and mind and breath.

Who am I?

I am William Burroughs, given the opportunity of arresting all previous assumptions.

I am Allen Ginsberg, in the matzo ball soup of time.

I am Jack Kerouac, writing an animal cracker poem eating animal crackers.

I am dreaming these little tinker toys of my feeling, putting them to rest in beds of prose and poetry. Making them wear shirts and ties, or socks and shoes, getting them to walk to the door, and answer the telephone and light a little fire in a brick fireplace in the West Village.

And a knock on the door. Herbert Huncke. Here is this man who has spent so much time around junkies, he has developed a very interesting sense of time, and in fact written perfect, though idiosyncratically punctuated stories of the life on the city circuits of the damned. But he is not damned at all.

A man who has learned and practiced the ethics of the streets, and refined them in his own person, and created art of same: short stories where you see a comb on a dresser, a mirror with half a face in it, and an overcoat thrown over an easy chair, and no one is going anywhere except for a dope score.

Waiting for Godot.

Precisely and quietly musical.

Mr. Life.

12

At Reed College, in Portland, Oregon, Lew Welch meets Gary Snyder and Philip Whalen, two fellow poets and students, and these three will henceforth relate to each other in much the same ways that Kerouac and Ginsberg and Burroughs are relating with one another on the East Coast.

These are the years of the New Criticism, an elegant classicism dominated by writers of the South, whom the poet Kenneth Rexroth once characterized as "the Corn Belt Metaphysicals." Their poetry was strict in cadence, and dominated by a language more out of the past (an Elizabethan, filigreed line) than out of the actual air of American life (touched with General Motors, and Buffalo Bob): a network America breathing in everybody's living room in television, live black and white studio dramas. Grace Kelly making her early entrances and exits . . . Captain Video . . . Howdy Doody . . .

Ransom and Tate and the others were holding onto something wonderful and beautiful, and did fine work themselves, some of it good reading today, but they made a difficult atmosphere for a young poet to make an approach into print. Everything had already been done, and done better.

The New Criticism itself made a clear case for one's elders and betters, and put it forth in prose difficult to fault on any level. But this has nothing to do with growing up to be a poet, and wanting to write a poem. This is something which is given each successive generation of poets as a natural right.

Now Snyder and Whalen and Welch did not huddle together in urban gloom, turning flashlights on one another's souls and smiles. They were out in Portland, close enough to a natural world of mountains, and ocean, of deer and vegetable gardens to let that be a kind of common denominator in their own individual identities. They were on the other side of America, with a lot of rain and smells of everything.

And Gary Snyder. Here was a small, wiry man, full of the lore of the woods, who would smile with a kind of complete, keen abandon, and be a sane and kind friend to Lew forever. Lew wrote Dorothy that he was one of the finest men he had ever met, and students don't usually write such things of each other right off the bat.

And Philip Whalen (like Snyder raised in Oregon), this was the Master of writing itself, as far as Lew was concerned. Gary and Phil were the peers by whom he would measure his own work for the rest of his life: Snyder, for his knowledge and commitment to the natural world ("the world that is not man," Lew called it); and Whalen, for his unerring feel for the word, and the line, and the poem.

Whalen, a heavyset, shyly retiring, and simultaneously irritably demanding yet charming man magician. Whalen writes exactly what happens, or if it didn't happen, it happens on the page. He is, in his own unmistakable way, absolutely a master of the whole thing. And now in the 1970's still only just beginning to be known (Ah, Emily Dickinson, in the perfumed summer air of Amherst, enough to make you happy and clear).

They don't relate with big telepathic all-night blasts in Manhattan winter (Jack Kerouac running around the block naked on a midnight dare: nobody there but Jack, and his breath smokey in the street-lit air).

And Lew spends a lot of time in the Chinese diner on the corner of the street where he rooms with a painter named Ed Danielson and has an early loft. He paints his room, and makes it neat for an affair, which only lasts a few months, and then another one, which only lasts a few months.

He is handsome, and fastidious, and a poet, too, but Lew sees women with a kind of ascending and descending flair. He knows his mother almost too well. These younger women have a hard time measuring up to the deeper intimacy of mother and son, and Lew is reluctant (probably) to let that occur anyway: getting in too deep while just beginning to be free.

Lew loves long hair; and sensitive, heart-breaking beauty in a young woman: the clear as a bell twist-of-the-head, the look of love on a new person. But he has known his mother all his life; and he has a deeper torment than is likely to be clear, immediately.

He enjoys being in love, and making love, but Lew is not too deeply interested in getting involved with a woman. He is interested, in that he has a feeling and a flair for the classical drama of life, and would be a poet Every Man as fast as you could say Blue, but there is another area of him that is a kind of open passage to his deeper self: and it is reserved for reading and writing, and for friendship with teachers and poet peers, chiefly Whalen and Snyder.

And he really goes into Gertrude Stein now: or Gertrude Stein really goes into his living and learning. He does his thesis on her, after studying her texts for months.

Gertrude Stein, too, fills that space in Lew left by the absent father. So, this extraordinarily intelligent man is finding balances to his own character make-up to make him a good artist, and at the same time fulfill his own uneasy, not quite resolved nature. And he's got an eagle's eye: a Turkey Buzzard's magnetized instinct for what will feed him.

He finds—he has already found—Gertrude Stein.

Now he has a Stein feast, reading and learning everything this writer knew about the written word, as much as he can grasp of it.

He takes it in as completely as anyone has, in fact. Stein atomized writing as thoroughly as anyone ever has, more thoroughly. Most writers at one time or another take a swim through the chill, bracing waters of her prose.

Lew put on a face mask, and an air tank, and submerged himself. When he came up, he knew what supported her structures: the sense of time, the ear for natural speech, and the clarity of a child's eye.

Lew Welch. Palo Alto, 1945. Just out of the army.

PHOTOGRAPH COURTESY OF DONALD ALLEN.

Hal Chase, Jack Kerouac, Allen Ginsberg, William Burroughs. Columbia, 1944. "We are acting as if we were International Debauchés as in Gide."—Allen Ginsberg.

PHOTO COURTESY OF ALLEN GINSBERG.

Neal Cassady and Jack Kerouac. San Francisco, 1952.

PHOTOGRAPH BY CAROLYN CASSADY.

Carolyn Cassady. 1944.

PHOTOGRAPH COURTESY OF CAROLYN CASSADY.

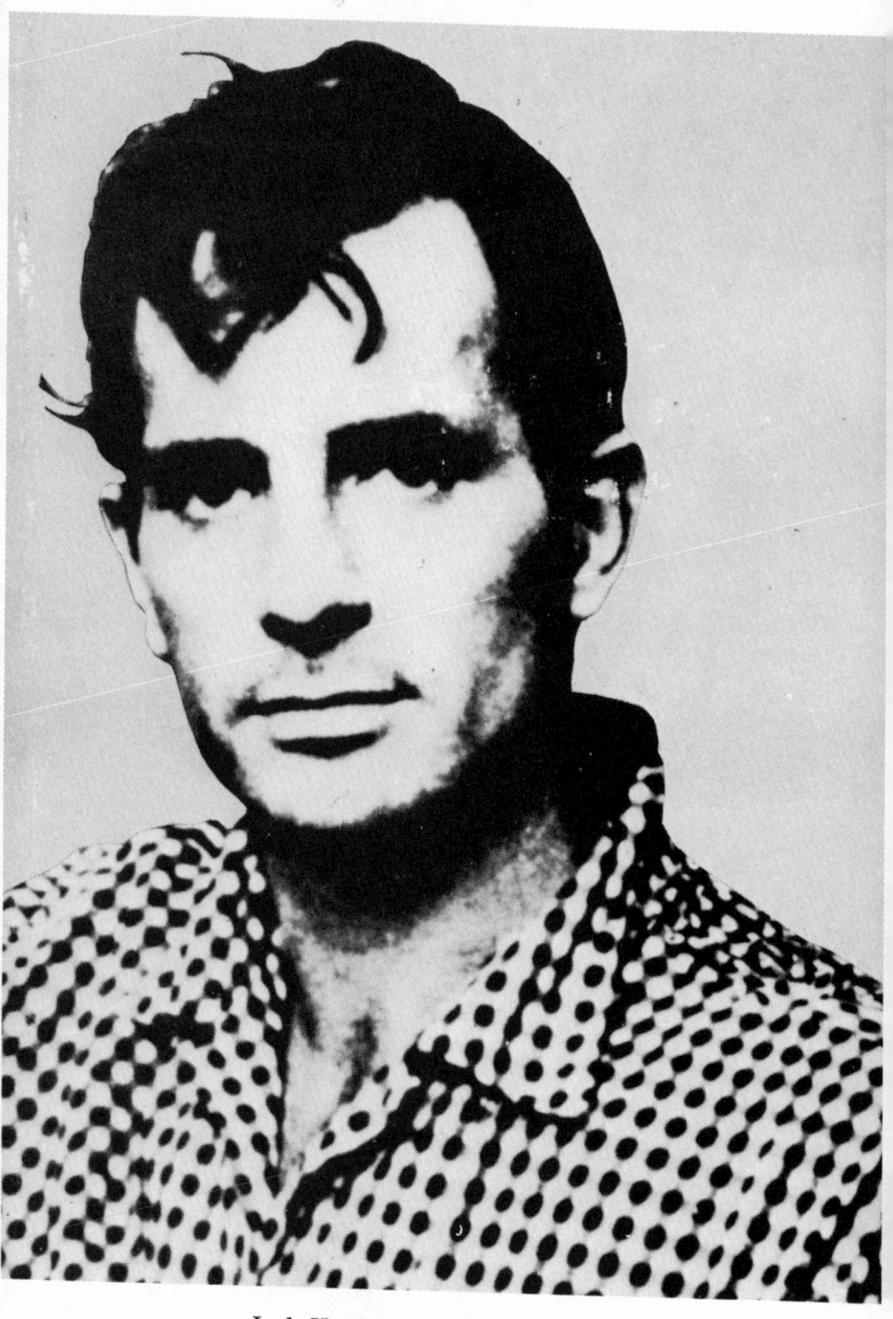

Jack Kerouac. 1957. "Success."

PHOTOGRAPH BY WILLIAM EICHEL
FOR *Mademoiselle*.

Allen Ginsberg. 1957.

PHOTOGRAPH BY HARRY REDL
FOR THE *Evergreen Review*,
"SAN FRANCISCO SCENE" ISSUE.

Gary Snyder and Joanne Kyger. Japan, 1960.

PHOTOGRAPH COURTESY OF JOANNE KYGER.

Lew Welch. San Francisco, 1961.

PHOTOGRAPH BY STEAMBOAT.

Lew Welch, Gary Snyder, Philip Whalen.
San Francisco, 1964.

PHOTOGRAPH BY STEAMBOAT.

13

And it's a Beat Generation sunrise the day Denver's Neal Cassady blows into New York City, with his girl friend Luanne, ready to dig and be dug—a friend of a friend of somebody's—but as history would have it, destined to plug in to the nuclear unit of Kerouac/Ginsberg/Burroughs plus others and it's now that this chemical compound combusts—that's Neal's contribution—and soon will take off on the road. Cassady is, you might say, the Midwest's very own Ambassador of Joy to this informal convention of poets and seers.

And John Kerouac, still a bit stolid in his command of the comma and semi-colon, and the great thunderous, river-deep mountain-high sentences of his first, now to be published book, *The Town and the City*, and perhaps even in danger of being lionized by the publishing industry into an early retirement to a leather-bound study, with a dutiful wife, three or four fine children, the National Book Award, the Pulitzer Prize, the friend of statesmen, the friend of Truman and Gore and Norman—but out of the racket, and off of the rock and roll and riot and riches of his prose written as an American nomad (although his mother always provided him a clean bed and good food when he needed to come home to sleep it off and write it down).

Think of it, if John never became Jack, and went on being a big Thomas Wolfe type talent, never discovered goofing along for prose surprises and bouquets hidden in secret typewritten keys, and wild scribbled notebooks of shirt-pants-socks-shoes, hello world, glee. That was Jack, touched by the angel and madman, bulging out of the Goodwill Jim Clinton suit, parking cars in a midtown parking lot for his money: Mr. Neal.

Now this is where it did combust because what happened was Jack saw Neal and listened to his wild, never-get-a-word-in-edgewise, spontaneous patter (make a sixties disc jockey sound like Pat Paulsen or the Great Stone Face): this man was a rapid, word chasing man chasing word chasing man chasing time chasing space—lookout! just like his driving—saved by exposure and the rare posture of ecstatic brotherhood. Neal was nervous. He was almost crazy. But he came for fun and love, or as much as he could manage. And Jack, who had recently fallen out of a short-term marriage, needed a life to lead as a writer about life, and Neal was willing to share everything: as they did in life, forever after.

And Allen Ginsberg fell in love with Neal, and they became lovers (because Neal wanted love and harmony and complete trust in everybody)—he was insecure and wanted love, too—and Jack was left wistful wondering about the deep day and night long conversations and ramifications of Neal and Allen in the Columbia apartment night.

The hungry generation.

And Bill Burroughs met the man and shook his hand. And Luanne got mad at Neal for always racing around like a lunatic, but he appeased her too, by turning on the great sunlamp of his attention and giving her a blast of it, undivided.

"Now, Luanne, we've known each other's souls from many different exposures and angles, we've swept each other's floors, and put away each other's clothes, we've enjoyed perfect love and communion in the sexual dimension, and practiced through the wonders of driving through America in my beat-up Chevrolet, rehearsed every nook and cranny of our Golden Love, and this is New York, which we have carefully planned in advance, and I do have the important responsibility of parking the cars for money, and seeing Jack and Allen and the others for the important reason (which we've also discussed and agreed) of making my own contribution among these important American men of the arts. Also, honey, I have brought some weed home with me, and it is better than either of us have known up to this very moment. Smoked it with Allen last night, and now must smoke it with you. We have important points to establish freshly, and this will help us. Where are the matches—yes, yes, yes."

Neal was like W. C. Fields with an eight-cylinder engine—and handsome. All the paradoxes and collapses and Atom Bomb and Christmas Tree Birthday Party, cop on the corner, all the magazines combined: *Life Time True Confessions Confidential Movie World Car*: is Neal.

Allen and Jack took a long deep look and listen into the whole American day and night in their friend: they saw the absence and the presence he was, and they both loved him and laughed at his child joy and handsome man purpose and importance. Neal came out of the Midwest to touch them with his . . . not his knowledge, but his *experience*. Neal didn't so much know it, as be it: he was the American fact, writ bold and clear in his own charged presence and haunted, yet ecstatic mind.

Ahab and Gatsby and Columbus himself (he parked with supernatural speed and precision, a car Columbus) in awkward friendly suit, and, as Kerouac once remarked in another context, slacks with peculiarities.

Nothing quite fit. The car didn't work—except it couldn't help but be fired and at times drive anyway under the enormous, comradely pressure of Neal's nervous system. This man really was worthy of much better toys, or deeper work, than the current social reality would seem to make available. But could he stop for a moment to make such a determination?

No.

Neal couldn't stop being Neal or he might perish in the extinguishing knowledge of the want and lack and crime and murder and sorrow in the lines of his own soul. But he rode the Life Principle all his life, keeping it together on a threadbare budget and honest work that blessed his deep restlessness with simple routines.

And Jack and Allen, who came from homes, after all, just said ah, and followed him into America.

14

By the time William Carlos Williams visits Reed College in the fall of 1950 to give a reading, Lew Welch is deep inside his apprenticeship as a poet. He is taking a daily walk and trying to make a simple, well-made poem about anything he sees which strikes him. He is paying close attention to the words themselves: yet importantly looking out for his material into the world around him. But he was more interested in the saying than in what is being said.

He is young (twenty-four), and there is still no pronounced sense of time in him. He is appreciating space, the textures and qualities of experience that give it its surface characteristics. A pretty girl, a swan on the lake, the campus noon whistle, the hair on a statue of some statesman immortalized in stone. Poetry exists in these qualities: that is, there is something of poetry in all things. Lew's keen eye is matched by a clear ear for tone, shadings, the weight of words.

It is youth he is inside of, learning a craft. Life will deliver its themes for his work in time. Right now, he is content to notice the way words play together in the voices of strangers and friends. He and Philip Whalen have founded a group of poet-students at Reed, and they make up poems out of words in the dictionary, testing the limits of what is poetic, until it becomes clear that any word will do, if you want to use it. They are all words, after all.

For a campus Shakespeare production Lew sets some of the lines to music, and makes a big campus hit. He sees himself making millions overnight, constantly in demand, being hounded for autographs. His mind can spiral like a Turkey Buzzard: shooting the breeze. He is easy prey for his own American Dream.

And then William Carlos Williams is standing before them—Snyder, and Whalen, and Welch, and other interested Reed students—reading his poems, and Lew is surprised, most of all, by the passion of the sixty-seven-year-old poet reading his work. The man gets carried away like a jazz musician, speaking and singing the lines at the same time. The words are American, too: native combinations celebrating the native air and mind and dream, full of *things* found in America: dimes, and wheelbarrows, chickens, and exhaust pipes, cups and saucers, and street corners, a bouquet of flowers, a slap and a caress.

Lew is letting this man walk right through his nervous system as if it is his own living room. He has not done this with a woman. He has done it with the writing of Gertrude Stein, and now he is doing it with the person and presence and voice of William Carlos Williams: this elder poet is under the young poet's skin, making a new alignment in his heart and brains.

Williams let the young man see Time in the old poet, and subtly, yet instantly, Welch saw the other side of his own practice—his art and craft—the side informed and enflamed by life, by experience itself. Williams was a passionate, old man, forged into an authentically compelling presence by the voice of his own poems.

Offstage, the man was extremely shy and quietly kind, suffused by a general love of humanity gleaned from his practice in a small town as an M.D., delivering babies and taking care of whole families. When you really get to know people, as you do in my job, you get to love 'em—he tells Lew.

And the young poet shows him his thesis on Gertrude Stein, probably one of the first ever written on Stein, and the old man gets excited. He sees how clearly Lew sees Stein, reading several chapters, delighted. A thesis on Gertrude!—and out here in the Northwest, of all places. And he tells Lew, this ought to be published—it's that good. Could you re-write it for a publisher and we'll take it to my editor, David MacDowell, at Random House.

Once again, all of Lew's sails go up in this wind. He sees himself as the "voice of the later half of the Twentieth Century," as he signs a letter to Dorothy about Williams. He communicates his triumphs directly to his mother: there is a deep and abiding bond between the two. They are like strange contemporaries in relation to the problem of Lew's father, the absence in both their lives, though experienced differently: the broken love—of husband and wife, and father and son.

Williams invites Lew to visit him in Rutherford, New Jersey, if he ever comes East, and Lew has already been planning a trip to visit Dorothy there, since she has enrolled at Cornell, going back to school to become—the mysteries are one, multiplying through time—a child psychologist. This woman who was not able to give her son the balance he cried and terrified her for because the father wasn't there in the house—was nowhere—is going to take her degree, studying children.

And Lew has in fact now graduated from Reed, and stayed in Portland over the summer, and then made it a point to remain to hear Williams. Now he has his mission to undertake. He is ready to get on the road himself, and discover America: going in the other direction than those starting in the East. He is a Westerner; Kerouac and Ginsberg Easterners; Cassady the un-named and un-tamed vast American Midwest, pivoting for some frame of reference.

So you have the dancing beginning. Ginsberg, getting released from a madhouse in Rockland where he went rather than jail because of a mix-up with the police over some stolen goods. (Someone he knew was responsible.) He has now spoken to madmen, and met Carl Soloman (to whom he will dedicate *Howl*) while incarcerated.

Kerouac has cultivated a musical ease in prose, traveling across the country, and down into Mexico, smoking marijuana. He will be rejected for *On the Road*, which he has written, in unparagraphed wonder on a roll of teletype paper rigged up to his typewriter. He is no longer Thomas Wolfe, nor John Kerouac. He is loose, and Jack.

15

A DANCE IS WHAT IT WAS, TOO. FOR INSTANCE, JACK WOULD wait around the Manhattan docks all day trying to get an opening on a Merchant Marine ship so he could ship out and make some money so he could come home then and write for a while, unhassled by money worries. He would sit in the big room with other seamen waiting to be called up, having quick conversations, getting overheated, walking outside to buy a meatball hero sandwich. A writer standing in the warm fall sunlight of New York, anonymous as any seaman. Trying to figure out the moves to get through life with the proper style and substance—nobody knows I'm the famous Jack Kerouac jotting down mental notes right now about this New York City dock reality in smells (of sandwiches, and sea-salt, and big equipment) and glad, watery light.

Two weeks later he's on board ship up by Nova Scotia: Geez, how'd I get my pen and pad all involved on this stupid ship, with nobody with any brains, all quiet and calm men of no talk and/or ancient poet wisdom (where's Allen Ginsberg, the crazy poet from New Jersey? and what are his Expresso thoughts? I want to know because I'm caught on board with a bunch of bores).

And Allen Ginsberg would be up in Cape Cod, deciding once and for all that he will never again have a homosexual affair. But be normal, heterosexual man, and delight his whole school of family and friends by founding a large and wonderful family. And in fact he has just lost his heterosexual virginity (or cherry) and feels wonderful: this a truly Wordsworthian moment of summing up and distant laughter of joy in the planets: I, Allen, now complete in marriage to the channels of life. He has made it with a beautiful woman on the block where he is staying for a few weeks with friends, a woman nobody understands, and everybody thinks is a whore. What whore gives a man complete life by being a complete woman to him, and opening the doors of grace, and loving him for his complete being. Allen.

And Bill Burroughs has got a little deal down in Texas, with some acres and a house, and has gotten married to a woman named Joan, and they have a large marijuana crop, and Bill is being a farmer, conducting farm life with quiet purposeful, yet relaxed command of the situation, and entertains some of the gang as they whistle through from time to time. Herbert Huncke right now, sleeping off a double amphetamine cocktail and mental somersault from the night before. Here's a guy who shoots speed and comes out into the living room to read a book: *The Catcher in the Rye* by J. D. Salinger, and the way he's laughing you'd think he was Holden Caulfield, instead of an old beat junkie with veins made out of shoe leather and olive oil and vinegar (with a dash of tobasco).

"You know, Billy, this kid Caulfield is cute. Say the book's on the best-seller list? You ought to write something like this, you old fart."

But Burroughs is in fact not yet writing—he will later write Allen Ginsberg long letters from Mexico which the poet will collate and turn into Burroughs' first book, *Junk,* later published as an Ace paperback original called *Junkie,* and if you turn the paperback over, and then upside down, you can read a completely different novel about narcotics by a different—call him Wayne Shirt—person: this is an Ace double giant. But *Junkie* is distinguished by this new kind of prose that was beginning to happen, and went completely beyond the current publishing standard and established principles.

This is a book by a very strange man, apparently the subject of the book himself. ("Rule number one, try to maintain a little distance on your subject especially if the man is a *criminal*, for God's sake! Miss Stewardi, is there any coffee! The man's a doper, and crazy, that's all. I recommend we don't publish this, J.B., in fact, I'll stake my life and my reputation on it. What's that you say—what if the man's a genius? Well, look at it this way, J.B., genius, I believe it was Clare Boothe Luce once said, is only ten percent inspiration and ninety percent perspiration, and tell you the truth, I wouldn't be surprised if the son-of-a-bitch *wrote this thing on dope*! I wouldn't be at all surprised. The man has no morals at all: it's a goddamn outrage.")

And a lot of other rules, lying like the contents of an emptied tool chest in the rain.

Because *Junkie,* which sold well in paperback anyway, has a kind of eerie clarity in presenting with no apologies whatsoever, but in a kind of faintly personable voice of simple precision, the life of a man (in the first person) taking drugs and committing crimes, and mingling with criminals. Burroughs has no regrets and this is anathema to the publishing industry. However, it did have a big influence on prose writing in the *next* generation, and as Kerouac put it near the end of his life, the book is a classic, kissing his fingertips in tribute.

And Neal is no longer with Luanne, but is getting together with a woman named Carolyn, a pretty blonde, and getting settled in a nice home in San Francisco, while Neal works as a brakeman for the railroad, and writes Jack to come out and stay with him, and live for free, and write your books, and I'll teach you about the railroad, and I've got this excellent weed (old Jack), and I know you can give me some tips in the literary dimension, and arena of words. You know you are my brother, Jack, and I'm your brother, you know too, as I can be because we have established an open field of clear and bottomless knowing that is in each of us, by letting be what is, and letting go what goes, and letting on what is on, and letting off what is off. And Kerouac is reading Neal's letters when he puts in ship and he says to himself, this man is the original artist of us all: if only I could capture Neal properly, I will have captured America itself, oh angels.

16

The poet in New York. Lew Welch selling ties at Stern's department store on Fifth Avenue. The red-headed, six-foot, graduate of Reed sitting in a small room in the West Seventies wondering over his life. Visiting the Public Library at 42nd Street and Fifth to see the Stein collection in the Rare Book Room. Taking his time over coffee at a diner on Sixth: the weekend . . . like a lost balloon, blue, over Central Park. Visiting the zoo—watching the seals and eating an ice cream . . . Madison Avenue, perfume trailing the clicking heels of women shopping . . . Lost in New York: without the sense of purpose the city is designed to contain, and exhibit. A poet in the magazine store, shopping for reality in magazines and newspapers. How do you see through what is to what is real?

The poet is a seer, in a way: he must identify his own species and its nature, and celebrate and refine it for his tribe. He must find out what kind of thing a man is, a woman is, and testify to the reality with his own life. He is in the business of discovering the truth of his own deepest nature. What is a man? Without the situation prevailing in civilization, without the current circumstance of having to make a living selling red, green, polka dot, striped, and assorted designs of ties, who am I? He must see, as a seer does, through the fabric of superficial definition which is imposed by government, and nationality, into the heart of things: the swimming center of the real: the nucleus, the microbe, the wave, the particle: and in doing so, in discovering the laws that govern his own specific nature, he is also discovering the laws of the universe itself, of which he is his own best, and most available, example.

Poets are so often frustrated, and snagged in their own enterprise: running smack into impasses that can stall them for life. The bitterness of the knowledge that such a true path is no longer an integrated part of society: that the poet's role itself, that of healer, essentially, has been fragmented by society to a degree that has endangered the species, the vocation, itself. The specialization of industrial society has specialized the poem itself: sometimes it has become no more than a machine, exhibiting its own process: this is poetry, these words you see before you turning colors and corners, making little show-stopping pirouettes and quick-change arabesques, this is the poem . . . While the slow depth of the creature, of man sitting or running, or standing in wonder before the seals in Central Park, is left out of the slick performance, is rendered obsolete in the poem itself.

The poet is an experiment with time and space, as every human being is, dedicated to the discovery of his own truth.

Lew Welch standing in his room at nightfall looking out from his unlighted room, smoking a cigarette, seeing a woman in a room, in a window, across the courtyard from him undressing, dressing, the female form, the soft and heavy flesh taking off, putting on the clothing of its given time and place. And his own tired flesh in another room, watching a woman whose name he doesn't know and will never know: a visual intimacy, the eye specialized by electric light, in the landscape of New York.

And he is hungry for what he sees, the fragment the city has given him to see: faceless, nameless, without a past without a future, the soft contours of the flesh unfolding in a window.

And then gone.

Maybe I should find out where she lives, and knock on the door.

"Hi, I'm Lew Welch, I was standing across the courtyard in my own little room, lonely, you know—I guess everyone in the city gets lonely; I'm from out West—and I couldn't help but notice your lovely form across from me, and one flight up in the window, undressing, and I don't want you to think I'm a Peeping Tom or anything, really, I'm not, but I thought, well, look, maybe this lovely lady—because I did notice you are very lovely—maybe she and I could, well, sit down somewhere, or go to eat or something—or I could cook some food in my apartment—and—just *talk*. That's all."

Lew turns on a light, and sits down in a big lumpy chair, grayish green fabric, and wonders over his scenario, smiling. Then, in an instant, the sad drama of the day—the hundreds of faces in Stern's, the meaningless ties which he is helplessly reluctant to sell—crashes through his nervous mind like a terrible weight of grief, and he is a young man alone in New York City, with meaningless and useless tears on his face, pitying himself shamelessly, without a leg to stand on —yet crying, and almost happily, nevertheless.

The release of tears; the heart breaking through the mind's stern proposal of locked and bound life.

God, here I am. This is really funny. How did I get here?

And then he performs a trick. He begins to see himself as from a distance, say the ceiling of the room, begins to look at the funny artist in the little Manhattan room (ah, Edward Hopper) with the sexy view out the window, gone all to pieces with self-pity.

And just as suddenly the tears not yet dry on his face he is laughing at the terrible and extraordinary fortune of his life: at, in fact, being alive at all—the terrible and extraordinary fact of it, because that is what it is. His mind is down into it, now, quite deeply enmeshed in the miracles of his own nature, eyeing the universe in his own mind's microscope: these gentle, timeless, sad, goofy feelings of myself.

I am alive.

I must take an egg out of the refrigerator, hard boil it, and place it on this table, so that I can study it.

I am the same fact: the seed flowered.

17

Becoming a writer is a long involved process in which there are numberless, almost endless rehearsals of style and substance—and the ratios therein—whereas being a poet is getting inspired and writing a poem, and then studying technique, and so on, but mainly being inspired. It's easier, in a way, harder, in another way, than being a writer. Poets constantly have to break through to the primary life, the heart of the matter, in themselves; writers constantly have to do the simple hard work of sitting down and writing. Jack Kerouac and William Burroughs were the writers of the group. The rest were poets, and then inspired amateurs like Neal.

Jack went to live with Neal and Carolyn Cassady in their San Francisco hill home, on a block with other homes, cars, and families inside. Everybody getting up in the morning for bacon and eggs (suicide and art unthinkable), and job, and school—serious and funny children, growing up in the world they never made (because they were just born a little while ago—like people born in 1960, unbelievable), and husbands and wives, sex at night or at daybreak—love in the afternoon impossible with kids, usually—and Jack entered into this house on this street, with his knapsack full of manuscripts, his accelerated literary imagination and craft, and his keen commitment to writing, being a writer, no matter what. Because that is what he was, and it was writing that Kerouac really lived, and when he wrote he really had a lot of fun. He had a ball, like a man making love or playing the saxophone making up inspired variations on a theme at Birdland.

This is something that should be mentioned because Truman Capote made the remark that Kerouac was not a writer, but a *type*writer. He made this remark on the David

Susskind Show, early in his show business career. Actually, the word he used was *typist*. And at the time the remark was considered interesting—a very sharp cut, so to speak. But it really doesn't make so much sense as a put down, though it is accurate insofar as Kerouac wrote on the typewriter, rather than in hand, except in his notebooks. And Truman Capote, presumably, writes in hand, although now he may use a tape recorder. There is less to say about this than might be suspected. Kerouac was preeminently and in fact religiously a writer.

He made his room up in the attic of the house. He would go up there with his lamp and books, and notebook, and pencil, and think and read and write and toil for his own soul and heart and for art and Neal and Allen and Bill. If there ever was a guy who was Beat it was Jack, because he was like Jesus in his surrender of his own American success story. John Kerouac was all set to go the whole route as a well-respected American author, and Jack lost him like a bore at a literary party, and went up on the roof to look at the stars and smoke grass with the bartender.

Or Neal.

And Neal was deeply flattered, batting big blond eyelashes at his soul-brother Jack, and wanted to share everything he had with this man, who made out his own importance in the confused and sometimes insane scheme of things. He loved Jack and Jack loved him, and Neal wanted Jack to share lovely Carolyn too. He didn't mind, and it would be good for Jack, probably.

And Jack and Carolyn had eyes for each other.

So Jack was like Neal's father, maybe, and Neal was like Jack's father, maybe, and Carolyn was like both their mothers, maybe, in a way, because that was almost the style for women to be during the fifties.

Getting the men their food, and changing their beds—and then (wonderful part) making love, which Mom herself was never allowed to do, though she might have felt like it with Dad gone so much of the time.

And Neal would go off to work on the railroad and leave Jack and Carolyn together at night. And Jack fell in love with Carolyn and they made love together and they felt fine, in the candle-lit Cassady dining room, with the little Cassady children asleep tucked in their beds, and Neal off at work, acting perfectly natural and pleased at the fact that they were, in fact, loving each other, and him, and drinking wine together as the traffic went by outside.

Carolyn was in fact a proper and pretty woman of her generation, maybe the woman Jack really loved, along with his French-Canadian Memere, whom he took care of all his life, and his last wife Stella, from Lowell, who tried to take care of Jack when it was already too late, in a way.

But it was already too late, right now, or from the beginning, you might say, in terms of Jack having the kind of clean and clear American success that might have been expected of this kind of personality.

Of course nobody could do it that way anyway. But Jack had the really inbred, suspicious, deep paranoia of an American lower-class minority group and he could have risen up on football-player-turned-novelist *Life* and *Time* kudos, and gotten the big firm American handshake.

And wall-to-wall carpet (which he finally had in Lowell near the end).

But he was also a Christian American Martyred Alcoholic Saint, with a real bleeding heart, whose mother had nurtured him maybe too well, whose little brother Gerard had died when Jack was a boy and made his heart melt in tears (Gerard a sickly and saintly sweet soul), and a father who had emerged as a betrayed ruin of American manhood.

Kerouac was complicated.

And he really loved everybody in his writing, when he was alone, and could be quiet and self-assured, and not driven mad by alcoholism and trying to beat Time having a ball with everybody, because he was a shy writer, after all.

But up in his attic room, by himself, jotting down notes,

copying exactly mental and emotional persuasions of his being, he knew—as no one else, of all of them, knew—that he was a peerless king of the written word of the heart's blue movie, love.

18

Lew wasn't a writer like that. Lew was a poet, and he was still, too, an apprentice poet, which is a complicated thing in its own way. The poet's apprenticeship ends when his life and his art become one, much as any writer's apprenticeship ends. And yet, this is a more difficult passage at times for the poet: words are a kind of spell for the poet to break through; and they can hold a poet longer in their thrall. Finally, when he becomes himself fully, the poet knows the language with an intimacy that is rare among writers because he has endured through so deep an awareness of the autonomous powers of the language itself.

He can cast a spell, at times, because he has endured a spell—of language.

And Lew had a very refined sense of words: of their weights and measures, pounds and ounces, force and relative transparencies. He had studied lines which moved by consonants (the Seventeenth Century) and lines which moved by vowels. He had a precise ear, good pitch, and a real sense of tune, or melody. He was very, very good.

So he had to virtually quit writing poetry. There was nowhere for him to go, and he hadn't yet acquired the vehicle that would make a new passage for him into the poem: time, experience, life.

He was a young man in America.

New York City—for the winter. Depressed.

And then with a classmate from Reed, Pete Oser, who had money, he went to Sarasota, Florida, with five other friends of Oser, to study and practice Scientology together, all of them living in a house together.

Lew explored his mental circuits: got to know his tensions, and pauses, his blind spots, and blocks. Whatever happened to him he had acquired the craft to translate it into words, in letters, in conversation, in thought. He was practicing, though writing little other than letters to Dorothy.

He fished a lot, providing the group with food.

He thought with the line taut against the sky: his rod and reel planted in the sand on its holder.

He was out of the dance of making a living—free again. "One sells his life for enough to sustain it. A sad thing."—he had written Dorothy from New York. Now he was once again among friends, rich with time and space, exploring his own currents.

Poetry, a poet, is the product of this release from the rigors of society and government and money. At least that is one way poetry occurs, through the benefit of free time. Poetry itself is a kind of free time, which may be why it is so seldom given a monetary return. Time is money. Money isn't free. It doesn't grow on trees, though poems (and plums) do.

How about Lew?

Is he happy? In the early 1950's, his head filled with Scientology, and the next moment, suddenly, empty, and delighted.

A fish on the line!

And he reels in a bass, striped with a strand of seaweed, and its own incredible, delicate iridescence—Oh, world!

Drops it into his pail with the three others. Rich as any American, and his father's son.

He stays down there—"Walden in Florida," he wrote of this period later—until the fall when he drives to Chicago in a car with his friends. Then back to New York, quickly, to pick up some belongings left there—and back to Chicago. The University of Chicago. He enrolls for his Master's in Philosophy. Then switches to English.

He sits in a class taught by James R. Sledd, the Structural Linguist, who dryly comments on and demonstrates his Southern accent, and continually constructs, to Lew's delight, endless and beautifully balanced sentences, talking.

Another teacher.

But otherwise he is less content with school than he had

foreseen. He sees through the university's Aristotelean approach: it seems to neglect exploration for the sake of order. He finds himself dutifully passing tests.

Chicago . . .

The winter colder than New York.

He works for the Post Office during Christmas Rush, delivering Christmas cards to Americans he doesn't know, his white breath in the air.

Who?

Gary Snyder had graduated from Reed, and was now at the University of Indiana in Bloomington, studying linguistics, and the two visited, and talked. Snyder is going to quit Indiana. Go back West, to Berkeley, to study Oriental languages, and then go to Japan. He wants to be a poet, not an anthropologist.

Lew knows now that whatever has been good about his poetry so far, there is something more important. Snyder is always a release to see, so centered in his own person.

The important thing is to be honest with oneself: to give up the "ideas" in favor of the real, to be—Lew. What a relief this is, as Gary says. The most important thing is to be whatever it is a man can be.

And then write poetry—to present this being.

But the poetry is the record, the presentation of, this process. Poetry is the record of this odyssey—not the odyssey itself.

Who? What? Is Lew. Is a man.

No American man can, strictly speaking, afford such questions. This is the poet's dilemma. It is not an American option. But Lew had started asking them anyway, along with the rest of the Beat Generation.

Beat . . . American dropouts: we give up. We come out with our hands up, and stars in our eyes. With our hearts in our minds.

We surrender . . . to ourselves, and one another.

Beat, in the sense of beatific, Kerouac would explain.

19

ALLEN GINSBERG WOULD WRITE TO NEAL AND JACK, AND then Carolyn, too, from New York, where he wanted to get away but couldn't yet—no money—being a copy boy, working in Market Research, a great background for his later work as the wizard of Public Relations and Human Understanding between all parties—Allen in the Merchant Marine —traveling in Denver (with Neal before Carolyn), down in Mexico—later South America—before he finally got to the West Coast, all the way to the end of the continent, ready to roll, and in these letters to Neal and Jack, he would wonder if they were talking about him behind his back, and if they still did love him, as he loved them. And when he heard from Carolyn, he included her in his family of feelings, determined that none should undo what was between all of them.

Allen Ginsberg's apprenticeship was wide ranging, and exhaustive in human contacts and communications: everyone (Jack, Neal, Bill, Carolyn, Herbert, Carl) lived in his mind and heart, and in his determination to see through his Golden Path of friendship and trust. Oh yes, this is idealized, and I should remember Allen the man, suffering the torment of this and that, New York City blues, shadow on the street corner under the streetlight, walking the streets of the Village and thinking about his sad lot in life, lonely, and full of unresolved energy: wanting a direct link with love and Neal gone with Carolyn. His youth really a grim urban doom, with flashes of insight: zaps of the new, peeking through the gloom, with flaming raiment.

I should remember the lonely man, young, waiting for the bus, stepping on, and asking for a transfer.

Washing lonely breakfast dishes in his Port Authority rooming house with a sink.

Passing hopeless cases on the stairs.

Going to work in the sudden gaga sunlight and joy (because a poet inside him is always waking up and passing out again) and he is the one and so is the sidewalk, the stoplight, the newspaper man, the noise of traffic. Subway ride to midtown: in the locked express with others ready for the American morning work—coffee break—more work—lunch hour —afternoon work—end of the day. The different smells of everybody going to work (strong colognes and perfumes, after-shaves): the great ritual unfolds in the poet's own universal and personal body. I'm going to work, hanging on to the subway strap, my body squeezed on four sides, if I get a hard-on I'm in big trouble. No I'm not, I've *got* a hard-on, but I can adjust it. This is fun, and important too, I know.

I love you, America.

He had traveled: by sea, by land, gazed into the foreign light and geography and heard the different sounds of other speech.

He had inside of him a vast literature of the heart, etched in sensation, etched in the real experience of his life.

Allen, like Lew and most poets, had a different sense of Death than, say, Kerouac's Christian Catholic vision, which was Heaven and Hell (Heaven): Allen knew it in the intimacy of his own body, the primal void of birth and death, which gives birth to everything.

Of course Jack knew it too, but differently because Jack wrote novels in which the effort is disciplined, and stamina is regulated (Kerouac liked to use grass and speed, etc.), and there was the urgency of effort and gain and loss.

A writer.

Allen had the conceptual center of the universe in his belly and breath (he was getting it located there) so that then he could inhale and exhale planets, and snow storms, windows, and paper towels, Mickey Mouse and Hollywood, tits, and cocks, ambushes, and semesters, toothbrushes, and Coca-Cola—the whole litterbug earth with Indians and business men and women giving birth, inside his nature, and available.

Being a poet.

He could exhale Chicago.

And inhale Bucharest.

Make a statement about the weather and go to sleep; dream of the revolution in human touch.

Looking in a mirror, see the story on page one, network television, the silver screen, across the country, and singing in the stars.

Literally see everything.

Because he has the cosmological eye: the male and female, root and flower, apple and tree and snake, Adam and Eve, all intertwined, like a telephone call with everybody on at once: a cosmic conversation with blood cells and bicycles, taxicabs and coconuts: the still blue lake making the mountain upside down.

It's wonderful to be a poet. And the key is maintenance. The universe is a big job, but this is where it pays to be practical. Take good care of yourself.

Remember not to get caught out in the rain with no umbrella. A smile will work, but it won't stop you from getting wet. Letting a smile be your umbrella is only OK once in a while—or you get confused. Let an umbrella be your umbrella; and a smile your smile.

Be an organization man without a gray flannel suit.

Organize the universe.

Be kind to everybody and everything.

Love is at the bottom of the whole concept: that's why it's got colors.

But watch it or you may become a saint. That's a certain color, too. Remember to eat well, and love with the body.

The heart releases a kind of pure oxygen through the whole body: it breathes wonder into all the cells. Love is very healthy.

Be a poet and save the world forever.
And don't forget to take a sweater.
Put this flower in the peanut bottle with some cold water.
It'll be here when you get home.
That's the way the universe works.

20

In the summer of 1952, Lew Welch cracked up in Chicago: "the whole boatload of sensitive bullshit" (as Allen Ginsberg wrote of it in *Howl*, his homage to and protest for "the best minds of my generation destroyed by madness") hurtled through his taxed, and tired, and nervous organism and he experienced the uncontrollable spasm of the mad. He walked into a stranger's apartment—trapped in the network of privacies, the personal booths, a city is—and started talking.

He had made the step from his haunted Manhattan room with the woman undressing across the courtyard—now, in Chicago he had taken his loneliness and disconnection and entered with it into the illegal precinct of a neighbor.

"Hello I'm Lew Welch, your neighbor. The windy city . . . Chicago . . . I was in New York for a while, then Sarasota, down South . . . but I'm from out West . . . and God, you know, my mind's got me tangled in the worst of all possible ways. I mean I don't know what I'm going to do next, but I thought I should come in here and talk about it. Am I interrupting dinner? That was stupid of me—but, you know, there's nothing outside of these rooms we've all got but movies and burlesque, and I'm convinced it's just not enough. We've been sold a bill of goods is what's happened. What good is a college education is what I want to know? I mean what good is it? We've definitely been sold a bill of goods. I'm certain of that. I'd rather go fishing—but it's getting more and more complicated. The fact is I'm a poet, but what good did that ever do an American. Do you mind if I smoke? Oh . . . I see . . . oh, yes . . ."

The chemicals had become too agitated, the yin-yang had gone into a wider cycle, over the accepted line of behavior. He was no longer in control.

And this was happening during the "tranquilized fifties" (as Robert Lowell, who regularly committed himself in Boston, put it) with some degree of regularity, especially among those given the uneasy task of remaining awake for the race, of trying to see through the tunnels, and mazes, of a civilization in which the mechanics had exceeded the necessity of our lives, and we were being dominated and even condemned by our own inventions. The Science Fiction mind of the fifties, terrifying itself with new gadgets: Three D . . . The Thing . . . The Blob . . . The House of Wax . . .

We were being condemned to endure a complete rescheduling of human experience: our routines no longer in any relation to the planet or the landscape or our neighbors. We had willingly locked ourselves up with comfort and convenience and suffered an immediate transformation. It was we ourselves who had become The Thing, The Blob, inside our private Houses of Wax.

The invasion from outer space—at least one of them—being television, for instance, which managed to contradict Time itself: by putting the same thing (Ronald Reagan personably introducing "GE Theatre," for instance) in a million different places at the same time. Our minds were being rented by advertising jingles that became interior mantras of meaningless gibberish: "Rinso White Rinso Bright Rinso White Rinso Bright . . ."

The civilization itself was turning into a visual and hypnagogic hallucination, and inside the city there was scarcely any way to escape it. Lew Welch was born in wider, more open spaces, and his mind was interrupted by skyscrapers and thick midtown traffic.

He was suddenly quite lost.

So he walked into a stranger's apartment to talk, speech being his gift and also his healing.

It was a kind of solution, but it hadn't been properly structured. Next time, he did it properly. The civilization had come up with the solution for him: he could rent a stranger regularly to talk with, to talk to—for a given price.

He went to a specific room located in the city and began speaking to a man named Joseph Kepecs, a psychiatrist, who was kind to, who listened to, and counseled Lew.

And this excitable, Leo, striking poet now began the deeper passage from his youth into the sense of time which one's frailty and mortality introduces: he was to see himself more clearly in Joseph Kepecs', and psychiatry's mirror: a friendly, and attentive silence which allows one to speak and listen at the same time.

A new profession for the industrial civilization: the psychiatrist allowing each man and woman to be his or her own tribal healer, wailing their own mantra of grief and joy, working through the past, the Devil, the flesh, Mother and Father, and the best and worst of times.

Which allows the man's locked and numb heart to open, for 50 minutes, to the light of a professional friend. Psychiatry being the specialization of friendship itself in a society in which it was threatened with extinction.

But there was a bargain involved. It came at a price.

Simultaneously, Lew Welch took on the job of being a copywriter at Montgomery Ward to pay for his treatment. He became a member of the society which had sickened and now would heal him: or at least maintain him.

This is the paradox of the profession of psychiatry: that it makes successes of men and women in the very society which has sickened them, and given rise to psychiatry.

Lew became an ad man for Montgomery Ward, meticulously putting together layouts in their Chicago office, which would then be run in newspapers in 500 towns and cities across the country.

That winter he composed all the ads having to do with television sets, which were read by farmers and pharmacists, housewives, and bartenders, janitors and executives, secretaries, and messengers, across the land.

At first Dorothy helped him to pay for it with money from her trust fund, but eventually Lew took over the whole financial burden.

Making do.

21

BILL AND JOAN BURROUGHS HAVE A MARRIAGE IN WHICH each is exploring a private chemistry—passing each other on the stairs, one blue, one green, one going up, one coming down —full of private narratives of blood and pulse, little histories of brain rushes and illuminated sleeps. They are a fun couple in a cosmic, and dangerous degree.

Joan Burroughs was tiny, and had given birth (despite so much miscellaneous and wild chemistry) to a baby boy, given the name William Burroughs III, who would grow up with his grandparents in Florida, and in the late sixties give us a book called *Speed,* which is in its own way a classic of the decade, comparable to *Junkie*—though chemically rushing, as opposed to the slow almost stop-time heroin type prose of the senior Burroughs.

This little family is down in Mexico, in an afternoon garden-party tipsy gaiety—in this low-cut country of brown earth and bodies, the mountains and hills like humps and valleys of Mexican bodies, the brown earth of deeds and omens—and here are these two special Americans, pioneering a kind of ancestral reality of speechless zooms and closeups on— flowers, a spray of yellow daisies, or dandelions, in the gone mind of 4 P.M. Yet really innocent young lives, maybe too free to go anywhichway, because there are no guidelines, just similar friends such as themselves—and who really knows anything?

Not Bill Burroughs, goofing at the party. He's got a revolver he's playing with, with real bullets in the declining sunlight, taking little sweat impressions off his soft fingers as he fills a cartridge. This is real life happening in the afternoon twenty-five years ago, which he remembers, in cut-ups and prose icicles later and later and later.

The newspapers are the real story of our lives, cut up like Picasso cut up a face—the way you see it without a camera, with your emotion in your eye, and something on the tip of your tongue, waiting to get a word in edgewise and maybe touch a breast, or neck or hand. We see what eats us alive: vision itself.

And Joan says, she's going to do an experiment if Bill will help. It's a party of expatriates under the volcano of time parted from American styles and ways: so one is a movie on the foreign screen of Mexican streets. In the Mexican zoo there are ordinary Americans looking at baboons, but they know it's not the same as where they came from.

The earth smells differently here, not as much money.

Being a movie of Americans in Mexico, a certain style that is not native, a look in the eye, and everybody is being each other like a movie star.

"What're you doing with that gun?" someone asks Bill.

And he gives his deep undersea American movie eyes of steel and penitentiary doors closing in the chambers of the heart.

"He's William Tell," Joan says, "and he's going to shoot an apple off my head, an apple from that apple tree over there."

And Joan is small, and chemically serene in yellow and green. The baby is napping innocently breathing in the atmosphere and mental imaginings which pop out everywhere—like a lizard's breath—over the kind brown landscape of Mexico, where people fly around at night in each other's dreams just like in America, but the landscape is lower—not big Empire State flights.

What a terrible responsibility, being an American. And Joan is ready to meet Bill and enact the primary drama of human life for the sake of some cocktail chatter and amusement, because the life they lead is this life, and you can't turn back a wristwatch even in Disneyland, even in the movies, even in Mexico—it's all real life.

Watch Bill.

"Awright, Joanie, you stand over there by the tree. Now wait a minute—"

And he rushes over and plucks a squat, red apple off a squat green apple tree in the garden, and a small group—all the party—has formed around the edges of this drama—people with driver's licenses and diverse careers, confused and quite clear, one enjoying the shade over there, in white slacks (the perfect expatriate gin ad), another over here thinking about dinner (hungry, like everybody gets), and Joan is tipsy now, a little weirded out by Bill because she knows he's got the *Daily News* in his veins and brain—although she loves him because he's just like her—and she accepts his apple, and tells him just don't miss you damn fool with her nervous system, that's all, and the revolver is hanging slack in his hand as he walks back the other way in his white shirt and khaki pants and silk socks and sandals (how sad it is we all dress, even in the most shocking and mind-ripping experiences of our beings: how sad, the carefully polished shoe of a dead person).

And Joan is trying to get the apple to sit on her head, and wants to take a sip too of her gin and tonic. She feels slippery and wants to get out of this theatrical noose she was just improvised—everybody waiting for this big moment.

And Bill gets to his position, among the breezes and light flutterings of leaves and clothing, a breeze with a touch of cool in the almost evening air, raises his revolver ceremoniously and takes aim.

When he fires for a moment nothing has happened, but there is blood between Joan's eyes, and then the apple falls and her body falls, upsetting the gin onto the grass.

There is a gasp.

A roar through people's feelings that does not surface on the air.

Bill had meant to split the apple, but had killed Joan by shooting her between the eyes instead. The American writer notices his own murder in front of him and the party of friends. There is no way the time can be reversed: the drama replayed. Burroughs' career will shift now: he will begin to try to undo the consciousness that brought him to this moment. He will cut up his mind with a typewriter and a scissors.

22

TALKING WITH DR. JOSEPH KEPECS IN HIS CHICAGO OFFICE, visiting him regularly for a period of nearly four years, the noise of Chicago traffic punctuating the slow delving into the red center of his feeling, Lew Welch was changing, opening into the interior of his own emotion—in which Mother and Father dwelled among the tables and chairs and wastebaskets of his earliest experience. His mother's incisive mind, and restless, unfathomed heart. His father's unaccountable (to one so young) absence, and then unexpected and too-brief presence through the green years of his childhood. Lew had the gift of tears, and would catch himself slant-wise in his own brilliant talk to Kepecs, and suddenly be crying in the midtown Chicago evening (after work at Ward's) about nothing, really, something back there in Santa Monica or Palo Alto across the continent, years ago—the sun shining on the quiet sidewalk outside the house.

Kepecs did him good, listening, practicing his craft, allowing his patient's necessity to surface through his thoughts as he spoke—until it would literally interrupt like a sudden enormous apple filling the room, the flow of talk: and Lew would see the apple, utterly undeniable, larger than his own body, and acknowledge his own gigantic need, the unsatisfied appetite of his life, and Kepecs would recognize the totem, though not identify it, until Lew himself knew his own need by name. He wrote Dorothy:

> Kepecs has become a real father to me—one resists the relationship, of course, but it finally happens. A boy just has to have a father to become a man—it's that simple. If you didn't have one, or you had one that wasn't capable, then you have to buy one later on. Or, you do what so many do—fashion one out of a coach or a teacher or boss or

what-have-you. You have no idea how important he is to me—it means that everything is going to be all right. Not magically, or perhaps, but simply *all right*.

And there was a kind of relief in this knowledge of his own reality: the apple, the monster, of his own ignorance of his need, suddenly reduced to its actual dimensions within the human world of his personal history. And Kepecs would now come out from behind his silence, since the monster had now come down to the size of an actual man, and provide Welch with the companionship, the simple fathering affection that was his continuous need. And in this experience, perhaps, in accepting his own need for affection, Lew's compassion was born, the healing instinct of the poet who has known his own sickness and been graced by a kind of deliverance. Having now taken on the full financial burden of his analysis, he spoke his mind to Dorothy in a letter in March of 1955:

> My analysis is easily the most important thing I've ever done in my life, and the thing from which the most satisfaction has come. I don't think you realize (because no one does who hasn't been through analysis) that one doesn't wait, breathlessly, until he is secure enough to quit. Instead you go because you badly need affection, warmth, and counsel—and when you begin getting it, it itself is a deep pleasure. It is not a patching job that attempts to send you off on your own—quite the reverse, it is a process by which desperately lonely people learn that they are not really alone . . . that they can trust people to supply them the friendliness and love without which there is no point to living. I say this, not as a reprimand at all, but to clarify a misconception that was shown when you asked "wasn't I secure enough to go only once a week?"—why should I deprive myself of seeing the person I am more fond of than anyone I have ever known? That is the way people feel who are being analyzed . . . People who don't understand analysis are forever wondering when you'll be through.

To us who do understand it, this is as absurd a question as asking a child who has a family he loves: "Why don't you go to an orphanage?"

In a sense, the liberation of emotion in this letter was the clearest possible evidence of the healing that had been done. He was accepting his own terms without apology. His writing was still another step away, but the principle would be the same: the release of his own reality. He had talked and practiced with Kepecs through Chicago time and trouble.

A year later, he had stopped going and was married to a woman named Mary Garber, the daughter of a Chicago newspaper man with whom Lew enjoyed spending time. He set up house with Mary in his five-room, spare, Bauhaus Chicago apartment, and they lived the ritualized dream of American life: Mary liked the role of housewife, Lew went to work. Mary gave him a wonderful present for his birthday: a rifle he had been admiring for a year in the Bean catalogue.

The daughter and the father and Lew visited the country together, and the father, the old Chicago veteran, was ready to run for his life at the sight of a deer. Lew said, look, it's not that way. You know more danger in ten minutes on the streets of Chicago than you could know out here in a lifetime.

Lew really loved this man, who had in a sense replaced Kepecs, and this might also have been a primary motive for marrying Mary—this father-in-law.

The next time he saw a deer, the old man wept. Lew could have wept to see him do it.

He was getting closer and closer to writing from within his own life, with his own voice, without qualifying himself. He had cut through his abstraction and into his own humanity.

Early in his analysis, he had written Dorothy:

> . . . an imagination which has only a narrow grasp of reality is almost worthless—shrinks to "fancy" rather than imagination. And if one is making works of art as a substitute only (that is, if one is kicking his ball and chain only)

then analysis might render one's way of working obsolete—but you will always, if you have any abilities, grow stronger in your perceptions and your expression of them.

In a way, what he needed now was something to spur him.

23

One day, after Allen Ginsberg had arrived on the West Coast, he walked into the painter Robert LaVigne's San Francisco studio and saw a large painting on the wall of a beautiful naked blond man. "Who's that?" he asked LaVigne.

LaVigne said he would introduce him to the man.

Peter Orlovsky.

Whom Allen fell in love with, and frightened initially with his passion.

Orlovsky was a young man with a child's eye and mind, a naked openness to the world, to life, bordering on a kind of benign lunacy. A gentle, tall, yellow fellow with speech that seemed to be the condensed issue of a mind in the midst of a wonderful association with its physical body, and the world at large.

He was always falling into conversations with people.

"Where are you going when you leave here?" the waitress asks one day.

"After we leave here," Orlovsky answers, slowly, boyishly, "—straight up."

Allen suddenly felt a new light, a new space—a yielding in the environment—after the dense strictures of New York. Space for his time, love for his light.

He was still troubled and working, though. He went to a psychiatrist, and told him: "I'm working at Marketing Research, discovering the motivation of Americans when they reach for a pack of cigarettes, so we know how to sell it so they think it's actually a tit, but what I really want to do is quit my job, and be a great American poet, and make love with Peter Orlovsky."

"Why don't you?" his psychiatrist said. (Psychiatrists really have done a lot for American poets, and poetry itself.)

So Allen did. He began to make it through the underground

of American reality, catch as catch can, keeping body and soul together with miscellaneous jobs—the weather milder and less frightening out here with little money. You can practically sleep outside.

He was twenty-eight years old, all done with America, and just getting to know himself, America itself, ready to roll, and in love. The clear blue light by the San Francisco Bay was inside him now, stretching his New York City nervous system with a new giving ease.

He was relaxing the tractor in his shoulder, the derrick in his wrist, the manhole cover under his eyelid, the pencil under his neck, the skyscraper in his elbow, the Third Avenue bus under his thought, the traffic cop under his buttocks, the Macy's in his thigh. He had started to see the moon at night. And lucked out to find a cottage in Berkeley.

He had met Kenneth Rexroth, Gary Snyder, Philip Whalen, Philip Lamantia, Michael McClure, Lawrence Ferlinghetti, and other poets full of the West.

He had a deed to do. He had to let Manhattan out of his bag, where he had had it stashed for so many years, letting out William Carlos Williams-like little crafted spasms of his anxiety.

He was ready to roar. He took some peyote and wrote a long poem with single lines that went on and on so that they piled up under each other—single lines three and four lines long—and he felt his breath and stomach and the passion in his maturing life, no longer young, touched with time, yet full of the crowning glory of youthful drive: a poem that rolled across the typing paper the way Jack's prose rolled, yet with the concentration and third-eye precision of the emotional all-at-once summation—"sum up my life, now, in this poem" —and he rose from this composition having changed himself, and by extension, the whole neural and worldwide tapestry of self.

He ended his apprenticeship with this kaleidoscopic vision: his Gemini sun blasting haloes through the urban doors and rooms and rot and shot of time's youthful experiment in his soul. He told the story of his own blasted generation of iron and mind and made the holes deep enough to capture the tormented and knotted heart. He came through the deep of his time holding his heart in his typewriting hands, free at last, of all the stigmas and striations, the rules and regulations, the points or counterpoints, of writing and the mind. He emerged.

Kerouac, in a Mexican hotel, receiving this poem in his own joyous escapades (Carolyn wouldn't come down though), wrote back, "Got your Howl."

Kerouac was great for titles.

And *Howl* was the cosmic birth of the generation, coming from all the way inside to all the way outside, so that we all could see again through the sleepy fifties just what a marvel this thing is that each is. It made an unstoppable front-page story of everybody inside the newspaper of the brain and blood and soul. It made the heart lift, and swell, with its own unfathomable awareness of the real in everyone. It spoke centuries and minutes, each word holding the rhythm of this changing, unchanging light. Allen's Gemini puzzle complete in its hundreds of pieces: a man, a room, a flower, a cigarette, the sun.

And the public debut confirmed the private conviction: it was done in November 1955, at the Gallery Six, with Kerouac hitching & hoboing up from Mexico and passing a bottle, and Snyder telling with a voice as clear and clean as a babbling brook about the way it is in the Back Country, and Whalen telling the way it is to wake up in a room at ten in the morning with the birds chirping and sunlight on the floor, and McClure telling about the elves in the sentences and exclamations that each self is, and Rexroth giving his own elder blessing to each new poet as the MC, and last of all Allen Ginsberg stepping up to read—while Jack shouted (drunk) "go!"—the big mandala of *Howl*, with the wonderful voice relaxed by the enterprise of turning himself so completely inside out—like a master of poetry yoga—and everybody knew it had done got done.

And never would be the same again.

24

WHEN THE BEAT GENERATION BROKE OVER THE NATIONAL media, Lew Welch was surprised and awakened and struck with the pang of yearning to be there, finding his old friends Philip Whalen and Gary Snyder right there in the news. What is this? Where am I? Why didn't I continue to bicycle into the stars? What left me out in this silly charade of being a normal American copywriter when I know I'm as crazy as the others, and sincere.

The Beat Bandwagon made Lew want to hop on quick before he forgot who he was and died an early death of unnatural causes, by closing all his doors and wearing a suit. He hurried into a newly revived correspondence with Philip Whalen, and wrote Gary in Japan—what's happening? It's exciting! Remember me, Lew, well here I am stuck in the American machine, completely undiscovered, and I'm wondering still what is it, this thing we call a poem.

He was ready to end his apprenticeship because he was so nervous and keyed-up and jealous and eager, he really didn't care anymore. He was ready to relax into being himself, because there was nothing else to fill the poem with, anyway. Phil wrote to him in a patient and impatient and yet greatly inspiring manner, telling him to get with it and forget everybody. Phil was washing lab glasses at the University of California in Berkeley three days a week, and otherwise just being himself, the poet of jewels and weekends in the quiet mind's diamond: the rare self everywhere out there, if allowed to be.

Lew said could you send some poems, I really want to see *the poems,* you know, and Phil typed up some short ones, including "Further Notice," so there couldn't be any confusion:

I can't live in this world
And I refuse to kill myself
Or let you kill me

The dill plant lives, the airplane
My alarm clock, this ink
I won't go away

I shall be myself—
Free, a genius, an embarrassment
Like the Indian, the buffalo

Like Yellowstone National Park.

Whalen's sunny Howl: his rare feeling for things (including self) as the bright toys of consciousness itself, breathing in his poetry, like worms aerating the earth. This one a definite show-stopper, which Lew immediately showed everyone at work in April 1957 in Montgomery Ward's ad office, and lest there be any doubt in Lew's thoughts, got an immediate response: requests for copies etc.—and the phrase "Like Yellowstone National Park" becomes an inter-office idiom denoting integrity in the face of insurmountable odds. Lew saw a poem being "useful" among troubled people, helping them and making them laugh and he was bit with the bug.

Good-bye advertising.

Hello poverty and joy, pain and language.

This was April. By July he had written a dozen poems that cut through all the rhetorical, Yeatsian superfluity and apprentice questions of the past, and started an original, Leo talk with the entire planet from his neat desk. "Chicago Poem," for instance, beginning: "I lived here nearly 5 years before I could/meet the middle western day with anything approaching/Dignity." He was talking now, and his language was suddenly inhabited by his life, rather than a squeezed version of himself between rules of grammar and precision choices. He was *on*. In the letter to Whalen with the breakthrough poems, he described his life:

> This is how I live: The alarm clock starts me. I have a hangover. I am nauseated all morning. The toothpaste frequently makes me heave. I can't keep down orange juice, toast, and tea. I chew gum and go to my car dressed in a suit and a tie. I fight idiots who don't know how to drive on a highway where thousands of cars go too fast and all the signs, street-lights, and policemen are confused and wrong. My car is old and unresponsive. Dies frequently and whistles in its generator. At the office I do the urgent, not the important. A friend describes it as "pissing on small fires." The meetings are not to be believed. If a tape recorder were put in the room and then transcribed everyone would think that someone like Perelman or Bemelmans was trying to be funny. It can't be burlesqued. It can't be told. All day long I am humiliated by inferior people who insist that I must do something in less time than it takes, and when I do they change it, making it only different, not better, so that I have to do it all over again in even less time. It never should have been done in the first place, anyway. Then I come home. The same idiots that can't drive are now as furious as I am. We try to kill each other for 30 minutes. Then I am home. I have a cocktail. I have 5 more. Finally I am back in the room. Dinner is served (delicious, Mary a fine cook) but I am so loaded and sick by this time I only nibble. Very insulting to Mary. All women deserve big eaters. All men deserve to get huge girth and to pat it proudly. Then to bed with good love if I am capable. Usually I'm still in a rage and/or passing out.

The questions were all settled now, at least the literary ones. It was a question of meeting everything with the rightness and equity of being oneself, fully, in poems and letters—and life?

The end of "Chicago Poem" focuses it; what to do with his life, his city:

You can't fix it. You can't make it go away.
  I don't know what you're going to do about it,
But I know what I'm going to do about it. I'm just going
  to walk away from it. Maybe
A small part of it will die if I'm not around
  feeding it anymore.

So he would go, requesting a transfer (and getting it) from Ward's to their Oakland office, almost breaking up his marriage to Mary, and then not doing it, yet, and leaving the long interim of his American experience, the single poet of his peers to really get in there and play, and lose his life, almost, in the complexity of the national will—and then get loose, and start speaking. Very clearly. His ability to die inside advertising informed his life (the ability to walk away, even from Lew). He emerged with a unique clarity, and a hard-won (through his own personal trial with the nation) compassion for the later villains in the gray flannel suits. He always knew both sides, and spoke up for his friends caught inside the mechanics of the American way, just as he spoke up for poetry to his friends.

Starting now, Lew Welch's poems were extraordinarily clear, the clearest of his generation, and even subject to being faulted by his contemporaries for their simplicity, but he was writing as much for the gang at Monty Ward (still there after he escaped) as for anyone or anything else. He wanted to help the way he saw Whalen's poem help. His apprenticeship delivered him with an open, an evolved heart.

Allen Ginsberg. San Francisco, 1965.

William Burroughs in front of the Burroughs building in New York. 1975.

PHOTOGRAPH BY GERARD MALANGA.

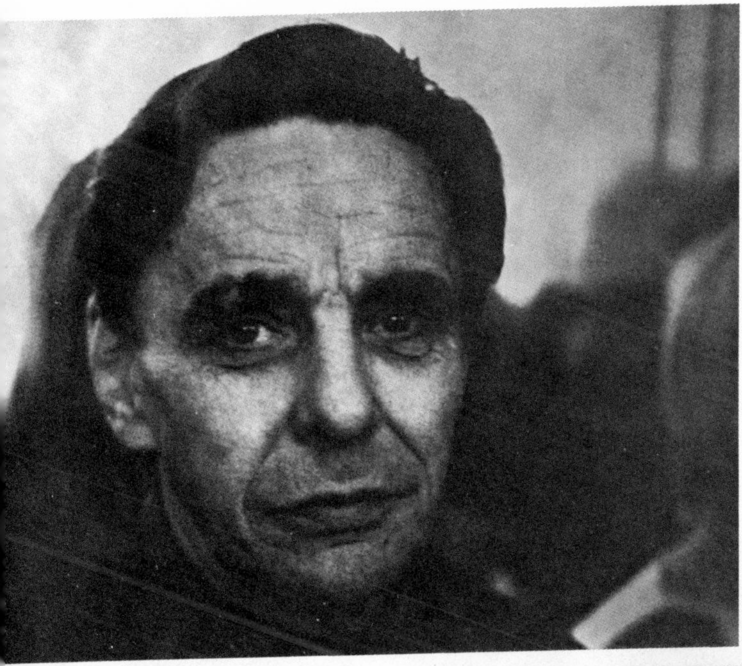

Herbert Huncke at the Gotham Bookmart. New York, 1974.

PHOTOGRAPH © 1974 BY ELSA DORFMAN.

Gregory Corso. New York, 1969.

PHOTOGRAPH © 1969 BY ELSA DORFMAN.

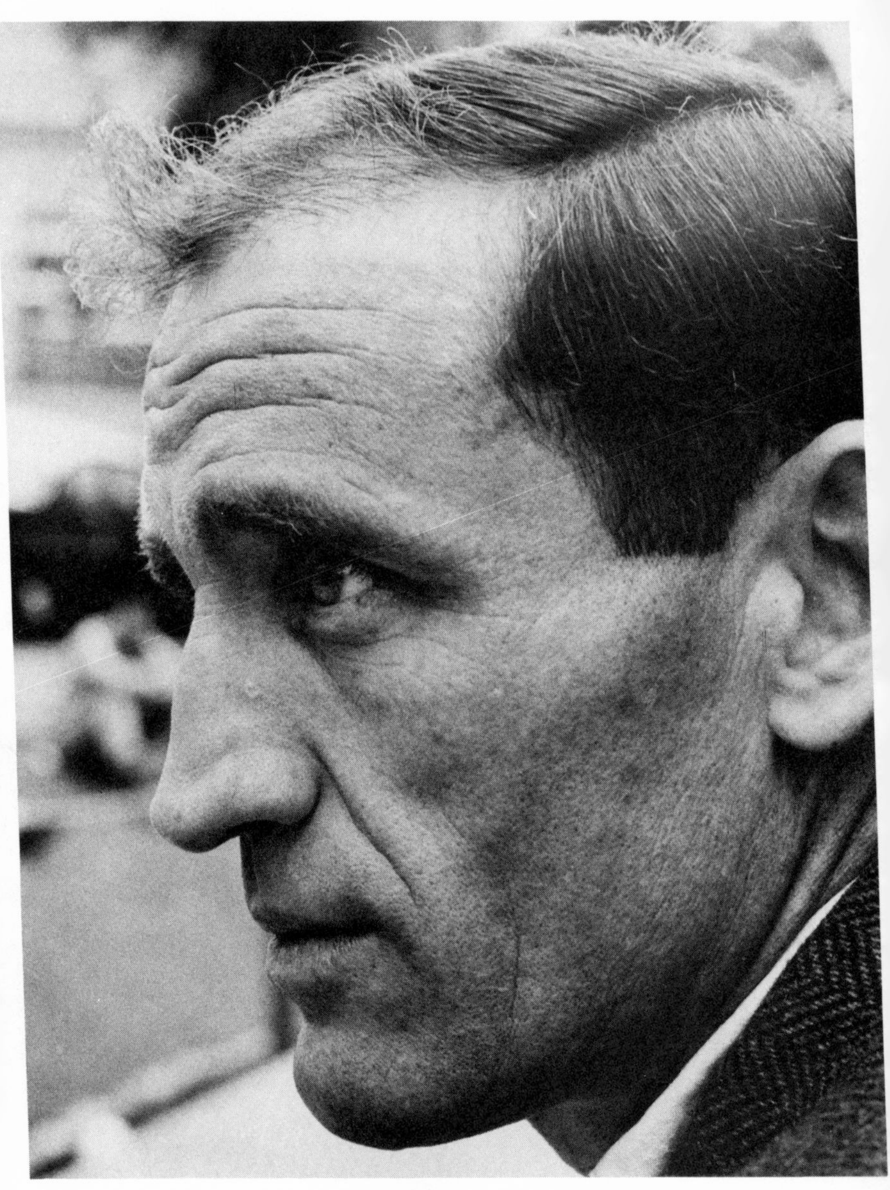

Neal Cassady. Oakland, 1966.
Waiting for Ken Kesey.

Jack Kerouac and his wife, Stella. 1968.

PHOTOGRAPH BY JAMES COYNE.
COURTESY OF ALLEN GINSBERG.

Lew Welch. Marin City, 1968.

PHOTOGRAPH BY STEAMBOAT.

Lew Welch reading. San Francisco, 1969.

PHOTOGRAPHS BY CHRISTA FLEISCHMANN.

Lew Welch's rifle. Marin City, 1968.

PHOTOGRAPH BY STEAMBOAT.

25

THE BEAT GENERATION IS FAMOUS BUT WILLIAM SEWARD Burroughs (who has been deported by the Mexican government) is living in Tangiers—where Arabs hold dark secrets in a different perspective on hashish—and he is hooked on heroin, and goes on the nod in newspaper lamp bureau window—and outside foreign sunlight—hotel-room, dreaming of Dr. Benway, the American empire permeating his simple thought patterns and practical understanding, a big comforting radio voice:

"You see, the man needs a new brain and there's no way we can fix this thing—"

His assistants listening.

"We'll have to transplant the extra baboon brain and see if he can make a go of it. Sure, it'll be hard, and he may not learn the difference between right and wrong. But is there any other choice. At the moment the man can't think at all except to say 'auntie' two or three times a day. We've got to do it."

His assistants, a team of white-smocked baboons, all nod in chorus.

Burroughs in the stop-time light of the heroin afternoon has internalized the entire nation and is playing it over his own junk-charged television set; a million laughs from by the bed with a hard pillow, and an uneaten tangerine. Who the hell needs anything but a regular shot of heroin. Every so often he types a scene—playing live on his mind's eye—on his typewriter, and there are discarded pages all over the room.

The Beat Generation will rescue this manuscript; and Burroughs will kick heroin and become a writer, employing cut-ups as novelistic procedure. First write the page, then cut it up—new juxtapositions of words like spoon nightmare and Harvey lab, becoming the interior monologue, weaning him of the American night-and-day mantra of madness. He cuts up American civilization, and the words make a new consciousness.

William Seward Burroughs kicks heroin on Apo-Morphine, a panacea that neutralizes the toxified nervous-system so the quiet man writes ads and comics for it in his prose. He finds a cause—the cut-up, Apo-Morphine; the mental and physical methods, respectively, to achieve, to restore, to awaken, sanity. He lives (as Joan has perished) in time.

Kerouac reads some of Bill's pages in Northport, Long Island, where he has bought his mother a home—Kerouac the famous author of *On the Road,* which Malcolm Cowley at Viking has turned into conventional prose, paragraphing, and making neat, ordinary sentences—still edges of Jack's ecstatic rust, though.

Kerouac is America's new literary hero, big faces suddenly poking through bushes in his front window—"Come on out, Jack, and have a drink with us! We're on the road, too." And disturbing his mother, and his work routines—an ordinary writer who needs to get work done, books on the shelves, libraries in America and all over graced with a new sensibility, and all kinds of people even outside the big fence he has to build. God, America.

Jack reads Bill's heroin spilled pages, and thinks, "This is the Naked Lunch: the exact moment when everybody sees exactly what's on the end of their fork."

And Bill agrees to that title, and conception.

Kerouac was the inner-office of the whole movement.

Allen Ginsberg meanwhile is rolling into Chicago with the public side of the show, the Beat Caravan, to raise money for a new magazine *Big Table* (why not call it *Big Table*? Kerouac had cabled the ex-editors of the *Chicago Review,* Lew's old school wouldn't let them run *Naked Lunch*): he's going to read *Howl* for everybody; Peter Orlovsky is along to read his poem about making fudge and having a bath and painting the floor; and Gregory Corso—whom Allen had met in New York in a Village bar with a sheaf of poems, and an Italian Aries street prankster glee—is going to get up and give everybody his own dimension of time and space and the old wristwatches of human faces.

And Paul Carroll and Irving Rosenthal, the editors of the review, are full of adrenalin and momentousness. This is it, after all. This is the biggest thing that's ever happened in America, east or west of the Mississippi. And Allen doesn't let anybody down, he reads ecstatically, and the whole show is a great success. "Why do you write so much about fucking!" somebody calls out.

"Because I'm queer!" Allen yells back.

Later he heavies Paul Carroll out, tells him to write spontaneously the way he, Allen, Kerouac, Bill and Gregory do, and Carroll with his heavyset Irish—tycoon-father—temper tells Allen, oh, fuck you, who do you think you are. But Allen has another side, the sweetness that balances his drive and public grasp, and they end up friends the same night.

"Was it right for me to say that about being queer?" he asks Carroll, who is charmed that quickly.

"Why, Allen, you told the truth. Of course it was right."

And Gregory is sitting in the corner with a beautiful young woman at the party, wondering should I get married, should I be good. Tonight someone passed me and said—important soup. What does that mean? A poet has to be a scout. And his poems should be beautiful colored merit badges about swimming and trees and north and south on the compass.

It's a big Chicago party with everybody's mind going on at the same time over the lake, in the night, with a beautiful white carpet, and flowers (zinnias) on the table, and short-stories and novels and articles and poems (by the millions) interacting with oblivion.

"I'm happy," Gregory says.

"So am I," the young woman laughs.

And out on the West Coast, Neal Cassady knows nothing of this but is going to work on the railroad, at around four in the afternoon, taking care of Carolyn and the kids, and a car on his street turns out to have two guys in it, who seem to know him and nod and smile.

"What's the hurry?" one of them asks.

"Drive me down to the station real quick or I'll miss my train—and I'll give ya some pot for yr trouble."

But when Neal gives them the joint of marijuana they arrest him and he goes to jail for two years. Ah, America.

26

Lew Welch wrote the classic slogan "Raid Kills Bugs Dead"—a line that characteristically emphasizes consonants —before he quit advertising for good in July of 1958, moved out of the neat wood-paneled house on Leavenworth Street in San Francisco where he had lived with Mary, and started making his living working for the Yellow Cab Company, and hustling pool across the street from the taxi garage with his fellow cabbies. He sometimes earned an extra $25 a week.

This was the break, clean and clear, and from here on he would take his life through phases and changes and upsets and onslaughts, breakdowns and breakthroughs, but it would essentially be his own path, the path of his own choosing, whatever the pitfalls. He quit America now, for good—to go discover America in himself, the poet Lew Welch.

Mary had finally felt that life was passing her by. She could see Lew was not going to be able to go through with the idea of marriage as she had envisioned it, and they split after this had been clear for a year or more. Lew was too restless. He needed something that would make him feel the urgency of necessity, absolute need—something far removed from a salaried job, and a fine home. It was over.

Driving across the Bay Bridge into Marin County, the day it was over, the day he had broken with Mary, he thought: "Now when I earn money (at least after I pay all my debts) it will be money for me to spend on something I need like a book, or a bottle of wine—a bottle of wine in a shallow rock pool of sea-water by the ocean, I want a drink—and I won't have to think about things like phone bills, and hairdressers. It's a great relief to be just me, even with empty pockets. I'm too crazy to be married. Being a poet, with no money, and no common sense, I need to be closer to the wheel of necessary survival logic—a logic of the body, not the mind. At all.

"Look at this sunset here. Here is something I can appreciate now, because I have taken my head out of American complexity—addition and subtraction, multiplication and division—all I know now is what's in front of me, and I drive the cab, and eye the sunset, getting to know my customers, and the drift of things out here on the coast again.

"This is me, and I'm free! It feels neat. I'm alive in 1958, oh yellow red sunset bridge diamond of my mind."

And he drove to Gary Snyder's little cabin on the outskirts of Mill Valley, where horses grazed in a field, and Gary, returned from Japan, continued his study of Zen Buddhism. He walked in and there was his friend, and Joanne Kyger, the beautiful young poetess from Vallejo who had the battiest ways. And Lew hung his ring—his wedding ring—up on a nail on the wall of Gary's cabin, and said, "Mary and me have split, and from now on I'm just a cabdriver and poet and I need a glass of wine."

It was summertime. Everybody laughed.

And Gary, who prized Lew as a brother and fellow worker, a brilliant man who could do fine things in poetry, who only fell just short of having the discipline that might sustain him into—who knows what, even—but a fine, wonderful man, good to share time with . . . who loved Lew as Jack loved Allen, Bill or Gregory—as all these people cared and shared so much of one another, because that is the real story of the generation and it is the real lesson of their time.

There was so little in the environment to nourish their own life, and this opened them into a deeper emotional reality with one another and made a change in the whole nature of America.

Gary said: "Well, now, Lew, if you need a place to stay, why don't you stay here."

And Lew said: "I was hoping you'd say that."

Jack Kerouac was back in Northport writing *The Dharma Bums* about all the Zen and life lessons he'd learned from Japhy Ryder, Gary Snyder, just a little while before when the Beat Generation was just starting.

Kerouac had little of Snyder's taste for the ritual discipline of Zen, or the woodsman's clean code of duties and responsibilities. He had finally ended up saying: "Snyder, I'm the Buddha known as the quitter." Being a novelist a different discipline. Which Gary cherished in Jack.

That night Lew heated water for a bath on Gary's wood stove; afterward got into a makeshift bed thinking and wondering with the noises in the field beside him, crickets, dogs, the noises of the trees.

Oh, how far a life is, how long the distance between this and that, and how good to know this side and that side, so that each side is opened up *inside*.

And Snyder awakens at around three-thirty in the morning, and it's lit outside with the moon, and he goes outside to piss.

Everything is quieter than Lew's heard in years: his ears have been doomed to Chicago and San Francisco traffic and urban be-bop for years and this now this is really *alive*, every noise activates the silence around it, like a person moving on a bed moves the bed-springs.

Snyder comes back and gets into his bed.

Lew says: "Gary, driving across the Bridge this evening, I realized that a day's work should leave a man with more money at the end than he had when he started it."

And Gary says: "Failure to understand that is disaster."

Lew thinks: "Yes, yes, it was, but now I'm free."

And his life opens in a new direction: he begins to study Zen Buddhism with Gary, sitting zazen, reading sutras, working around the cabin.

Once when Snyder rings the bell to signal the end of sitting meditation Lew hears it with his whole body—it rings his very bones.

As the marriage ring had, differently.

He hears the sound as if it were a nameless, pure pronunciation of the universe inside and outside. His mind is gone in that instant, and his consciousness pure: the mind a noun, and consciousness a verb.

The bell rings inside Lew when it rings outside, which is what Zen is.

27

Jack Kerouac had been handed—after the endless toil of his youth and into his middle thirties—the whole American solar system: he had become a star in the firmament of its avid and deep dream. Teen-agers dreamed of Jack with his thumb out on the highway, out there discovering America, living for this moment, the now, the fire on the end of the mind's eye—a cosmic cowboy of the American highway. Kerouac had burned himself deep into the iconography of the American mind: along with the double-line down the highway forever. He was a new frontiersman, seeking kicks instead of claims. A guy with a wired mind, ready to tell the big story of everything to everybody, somebody like somebody you know, a real American movie star.

Except Jack was beat, bent, drunk, clunked, tottered, clobbered, aged, glomed by Mexican gloom and Lowell doldrums, hummed by marijuana, zoomed by speed, lettuced by lettuce fields passing in the night, opened by space and time, into a transparent pilgrim with one grim word occupying his pied mind. And the word was—plastered—Death.

Because Kerouac had to do a lot to slow American time down in prose so that it would admit a little of the right brain hemisphere after the logistics of the hip practitioners of post-Hemingway and postcard Fitzgerald, the big singularities of brains trained like hair at Harvard, and Princeton and Yale.

Oh, this old fool Jack, you see, had doubled up on the page and given a completely new flavor into writing, and nobody could afford to do that without giving all kinds of pounds and ounces of flesh and spirit, soul and mind into the American bargain. You make a bargain with America, one way or the other, and Jack had put himself whole on the line to open the hemispheres of his heart. "Accept loss forever," he wrote in his Essentials of Spontaneous Prose. He lost to win, like any angel saint of time, martyr of the colorful array of space's movie and cartoon.

Jack was no longer out there with his lumberjack shirt and crucifix. He was at home with his bottle and typewriter and his mother trying to take care of him, and his shoes in the closet, and his clean bed, and the moon shining in his attic window. "Yippee, I'm a writer, and I'm drunk on being time's transcriber like Proust on the run. I'll telephone the story to Heaven if I can remember it right in the Mexican night."

And then that easy-going television stylist and piano-playing American, Steve Allen, asks Jack to fly out to the coast and do him a favor and do his Sunday night TV show (opposite Ed Sullivan) so that millions of Americans can see Jack and hear him read his beautiful words to Steve's sensitive piano shading. Steve and Jack had done a beautiful album together just so.

And so the old trooper, who has now deluged the nation with joyous spontaneous bop prosody—all kinds of companies bringing out his old manuscripts, one after another, and with their original punctuation now that he's famous, so some of the best like *Tristessa* are Avon paperback originals which nobody even reviews although it's superb—he goes all the way out to the coast, for a quick dip in the media with Steve. Then head up to Frisco and be a joy with old friends, new friends, everybody in town.

The night of the big Sunday night network show—and everybody's tuned in to get a look at James Dean in prose, the guy who knows the American night like the map on his hand—Jack gets a little boozed up across the street, but then reads with a big spirit and vocal authority coming through the opened though not too mobile expression on his face—and America gets it right through the TV—a little drunk. But good.

And Steve Allen does the piano back-up nicely like on the

record. A great jazz reader Kerouac is when he gets going. America sees.

Then Jack's up in Frisco with the boys at City Lights. Lawrence Ferlinghetti with gentle and comradely curiosity about the rabble-rouser, Phil Whalen, and McClure, and Lew Welch pulls in suddenly with a Willys Jeepster his mother has given him as a present in Reno, and he's driven back in a hurry to meet Jack.

And makes his car the taxi to oblivion and absolute conversational sunlight in the Frisco fall of the drinking party. Lew's living at East/West House, a commune of (mostly) students of Buddhism. But Jack wants to get back to his Northport attic/studio before Thanksgiving, and Lew and Albert Saijo, who also lives at East/West, a rare Bay Area Japanese Dharma explorer, decide to go there. Lew will drive Jack back in the jeep, Willy, which he loves—and Albert will accompany.

The three go on the road one morning in San Francisco North Beach urgency of momentous morning of our lives (we are three people in the world of time, money, love, and gasoline). It's special—all across the huge, rolling American sunlight, starlight, dark and light studded land.

Albert, lying in the back, noticing special, nothing special roadside items.

"I saw a handkerchief outside Reno, lying in the dust."

"I saw a comb at twilight on a mailbox in a little town I never knew existed . . ."

"I saw a woman in a telephone booth talking to her lover outside the diner, a thousand miles from there."

Three whizzes.

Then it's understood that nobody in America wipes their ass properly; should be done with soap and water. Everybody's got a dirty ass.

"The President's got a dirty ass!"

"So does the Secretary of State!"

"Everybody in Congress has one, too."

When they get into New York, Kerouac takes the two on a tour and they are photographed with Jack by Fred McDarrah for the picture book, *The Beats,* all of them writing haiku at McDarrah's Village apartment: important.

28

Lew Welch's continuing dilemma was how to remain a poet and at the same time support himself, a tricky question, subject to the subtle evasions of the muse, or the tiredness of the body (though Lew tended to feel the tireder the better in certain instances: less resistance to the real). During the summer and fall of 1961, he worked as a salmon fisherman with a friend named Bill Yardas: going out in the boat for several days, getting a big cargo of salmon (keeping it on ice), and then delivering it into San Francisco to get the money, sleep for a couple of days at East/West House, where he and the poetess Lenore Kandel were now living together, let off a little steam, and then back to work.

On the boat, he'd be up before dawn, pissing into the ocean, then down in the cabin getting the radio going while Bill got some eggs and potatoes cooking, hot coffee, and he'd play with the dial to tune in the Italians, the only salmon fishermen who went out every day from dock, so they'd give each other weather reports of the various areas as they passed them—after first giving the news of last night's lasagna and veal rollatina. A great morning ritual, the Italians on the radio: "Gregory, wonderful pasta last night. Point Reyes seashore drizzling. What's your cousin's name?" Like the palm tree full of sparrows he used to wake up under years ago in Florida. God, what a life. I'm getting old. My knife slipped yesterday again—my hands are so swollen.

Hemingway should have hunted this way. This old boat is quite a tool, hauling us, and holding sway over these stocks of salmon—the man and the boat, together, make the catch. If only he had hunted to make a living he might have seen the whole spectacle differently: the way an Eskimo does, who hunts for survival, with the depth and skill of a vital interaction with the environment.

Even Whitman just watched the workmen, idealizing their enterprise. But I *am* a goddamn workman. I *know* what the work is—and it's beautiful sometimes, like a dance, but still hard work—for money to eat and live, that's all.

And he and Lenore, on shore, were happy and then unhappy. Lenore was a great life-mate in a way for Lew, though she didn't share the fastidious nature of his mind, his sense of how things must be and work, in life and home and a relationship. And Lew might have wanted her more committed to honoring some kind of tacit marriage vow: he wanted to have his world clearly in tow, and Lenore was a free spirit, and generous and outward in her life: the very opposite of Mary, in a way.

They moved into a new suite of rooms at a new East/West House on Geary in the winter of 1961–62, the salmon season failed (they had been just getting by), and in the spring of '62, Lew and Lenore, tearfully, split up. Lew was all in pieces again—in pieces and pieces, because Lenore was good to him, and beautiful, and he still couldn't do it, somehow.

He even went to a psychiatrist again, for a few visits. He was told that he had trouble accepting love.

Then Lawrence Ferlinghetti, seeing Lew was in a bad way, let him have his Bixby Canyon, Big Sur, cabin for a couple of weeks to cool out, because Lew was close to committing himself. His head was reeling: it was information overload, backed up traffic in the mind, and a huge, honking madness of the heart. He left San Francisco.

And now he sat, and stood, hiked, cooked, and slept in the huge landscape of Big Sur, and realized his whole being was held so tight it was like a fist: trying to make a living, trying to keep loving, trying to be a poet in the unholy madness of the world, as he had known it all along.

And after about a week in the cabin, one morning, he looked into the clear stream where he got his water, and he saw his own face—"a ring of bone/in the clear stream/of all of it."

And he knew then that he was unclenching, again, as the

poet must do over and over and over again, in his life, to be a poet, to go on receiving poetry—that he must keep on breaking through the terrible locks and blocks and forts and platoons and cavalry and militia and bombs and bullets that continually seem to accumulate in the physical reality of a man in the society we are inside of. The poet must continually open again amidst the crashes and sonic booms, the thunderous cacophony of modern life, as if he were, simply, a flower on a quiet hillside in the sun—to take in the essence and the message of the real world, the wordless one that is out there all the time, if we can stop the racket of our own mad mind and time and place.

And Lew could feel his tired and sad and alcoholic and bruised and battered body and spirit, heart and soul, opening itself—once more—timidly, almost sullen, scared and tentative; as a trout just taken off the hook, and put back in the water, will remain still and simply breathe in the water for a few moments, before re-entering his swimming life. And Lew was suddenly crying—crying and crying. The gift of tears had been waiting to release a flood tide to wash through all the corridors of his being, to drench him with his own human sorrow: the lost man, once again finding his own center in the world, his own center in his heart.

And Lew knew then that his own job, in a sense, was to constantly, vigilantly, keep himself open—and he understood the suicide of so many poets faced with this task, and the resistant and battle-scarred self, remaining closed. He knew he might someday die that way himself, if he could find no way through himself again, and back into the real, opening the whole mess of doors a human being is, and letting it all flow through. And then, suddenly, he heard the words "ring of bone" where "ring is what a bell does." The mandala suddenly turned into a mantra—which is, in a sense, the exact moment of poetry.

29

In a certain sense, Lew Welch's descent into the alienation and despair of an American outlaw/loser—because that is what he became, almost exactly, when he chose poetry over advertising—is indistinguishable from his ascent to the summit of his own art as a poet. The farther afield he went in terms of the society of his time, the more remarkable and authentic was the poetry that came out of his life.

At the age of thirty-six, after experiencing the breakdown and luminous vision of himself in the clear stream at Bixby Canyon, in the fall of 1962, Lew Welch made his way to the north country of his native California, a place called Forks of Salmon, on the Salmon River, and he slept out under the stars, and in the mornings typed letters to his friends Gary Snyder and Joanne Kyger in Japan, Philip Whalen in San Francisco, with his typewriter on top of his footlocker: F. Scott Fitzgerald in the wilderness, trying out life all alone among the coons, and deer, and squirrel, the stars and the river.

I've lived all my life with half my mind square and snobbish as F. Scott Fitzgerald, he was to write Whalen, and I've finally decided to get out of the city for good: only out here am I not frightened and crazed. He hung around to beg a cabin for the winter, and quickly got one through the friendly assistance of local people. A thousand feet up, in a meadow reached only through a two-mile climb, he found a cabin built by an old Wobbly who had never claimed the land he built it on, and then died. He wrote of the cabin to his friend, the poet Kirby Doyle:

> [It] was made by a craftsman such as the world will probably never see again. The door and window frames are made of oak planks apparently split, not sawn, from native

> oak. It has rained continuously for 5 days and not one drop has leaked in. The inside is all golden with the natural woods, and criss-crossed with delicate bracing. It is like living in a Vermeer.

He named the cabin Rat Flat:

> Horrible infestation of rats. Rats scampering over face, clawing at old shakes, nervously scuttling like mad things. No sleep at all for 2 nights. I went mad one night, leaped out of the sleeping bag and pounded the walls. My only light, a kerosene barn lantern, showed many little faces staring down at me from the rafters: not frightened, bemused at my antics. By this time I had dozens of little sardine cans filled with poison pellets. "Eat! Eat!" I screamed, vowing traps, guns, unspeakable tortures. Then I went after one with a hammer and broke the handle.
>
> Now all of them are dead, the last one trapped, all the rest poisoned. And I miss them!! They were mountain pack rats, gray with snow-white bellies and white feet. They collect everything. In the enormous nests I found after tearing out the canvas ceiling I found shaving brushes, toothbrushes, .22 cartridges, pencils, and a small calendar I am now using.

But Lew couldn't make the climb after a while. His mailbox was two miles down, two miles up again, and he ended up abandoning Rat Flat to the ghost of Lawrence Meyer, the man who built it, even though he knew it was the ideal place for a tormented poet like himself to live. An old man who lived right on the river told him he could stay in an old CCC shack on his property, and Lew ended up living there instead —nowhere near as beautiful, but more convenient.

Sometimes he wouldn't see or speak to anybody but a skinny little cat he adopted and named Stanley, for days at a time. And he started writing the poems he called "Hermit Poems," which are among the very best that he ever wrote: full of the feeling of life on the river, with the wild animals, and his little cabin, and a small garden he kept, and a bottle of whiskey often, and his heritage among the sages of ancient times who also lived alone, and wrote funny lines about the way it is where nobody is. Lew Welch found something closer to a home at Forks of Salmon than he had ever known. The people all took to him right away—The Bennets down the way mending his broken chain-saw, and giving him a gallon of fresh milk from their cow one afternoon.

Oh, home—away from home. A simple way for a poet to go.

Gary wrote enthusiastically from Japan, because Gary knew those joys, too.

And every so often Lew would make a holiday foray into the city of San Francisco, and get totally stoned and bagged and plastered and gassed, and come back and lay out again.

Do zazen in a certain spot with his rifle across his folded (lotus) legs, and the deer would come up and graze right in front of him, and he wouldn't shoot them, because he usually didn't need the food. He fished a lot, and his mother, Dorothy, was sending him $100 a month.

Dorothy did what she could: and this was all Lew really needed, except he had discovered another hermit like himself, but a painter, living in a cabin a few miles away, a wonderful guy named Jack Boyce, and they would get together and drink and straighten out the problems of the world, before passing out. So by the end of the month he'd usually run out of money drinking.

But he had everything, really, except a woman, and he'd more or less come to the conclusion that he really didn't work right with a woman, anyway. He really was a hermit in his heart, although he loved a good time, and staying up all night and getting into a conversational whiskey diamond complexity and heart and soul feast.

Then to be alone—in the woods, with the wood stove fire in the cabin. Stanley used to wake him up each morning by coming and sitting on his chest and purring. Wake up, Lew. OK, Stanley, howaryou, old buddy.

Then one morning Stanley wasn't there, and Lew heard a squeak from the porch, and got up and opened the door and there was Stanley with two legs gone, and the skin on his back hanging from him like a pelt, and Lew went, oh my God, and brought him in, the poor little cat ravaged by a predator that didn't even want to eat him, just mess him up, maybe a gray squirrel, Lew figured, and then before he knows it, little Stanley's purring, like, I'm saved, Lew, I'm home, you got me, now it's OK.

But Lew's neighbor, the old man who's now told him he can stay as long as he (the old man) lives, says: "Well, really, you could take him to a Vet in Yreka, but you know with his two legs gone like that, he's gonna have a hard time of it, you know, like I don't see how he could really make a go of it without legs like that, so if I were you I'd shoot him, you know? What else can you do?"

And he goes back to his cabin and loads his rifle, and he looks at Stanley, and Stanley looks at him, and Lew thinks well, there's no way I can do this while Stanley's looking at me, that's for sure.

And Stanley looks right at Lew while he's thinking this, and then he looks away—as if he has read Lew's mind, and knows exactly what he's going to do, because he's seen him use the gun.

He looks right at Lew and then he looks away.

And Lew shoots him.

And then he carries him outside to the garden and buries him, the little battered body of Stanley, all gone.

And he thinks, now I know how it is somebody shoots himself: he pulls the trigger when he's not looking.

And then Lew goes on a three-day drunk, because he really loved that little cat.

30

AND EVERYBODY GETS TO GO TO HEAVEN—NEAL, JACK, LEW—at the end of the sixties—crazy decade with a hall of mirrors laughing death-rattle sphinx in the American mind—and the beginning of the seventies—May of '71, Lew—a new decade where everything is neat and in place (Lew would have liked it, oh) like the wood for the fire, nothing at all like a revivified fifties (Happy Days number one on TV, though) but a serious, sane attempt to make sense of the steps of life, like childhood—but first birth, Birth—and all the way to Death, a whole experience, too, not to be slighted, or avoided.

Well, Lew approached this particular moment, this experience, as if he had been training for it all his life—and of course being a poet, he had: poets live in the unity of the principles of experience, life and death, or life-death, sleeping and waking up, hello and good-bye, night and day, yes and no, and Lew had done a lot of playing around the corners and borders of these forces, flirting with extinction, flirting with immortal insight: his mind was a keen instrument, his eyes were very very sharp and he was always ready to get his life into some massive marriage with a BIG reality: like being a poet, or being an advertising man, like living in Chicago, or getting psychoanalyzed, not to mention getting really far into the writing of Gertrude Stein (letting Stein step right into his mind, and sit down and take over), or being an alcoholic, or being a Zen Buddhist—Lew touched a lot of bases, but it was only at the end (and in a way, the rest was a kind of exhibition game for the real thing)—only in the end, that he did it all, hit the ball out of the park, made the immortal poem, the home run.

He did the last thing he did perfectly. He needed the biggest of all the big mysteries to pitch him the fast ball, the way

America pitched him the original Birth without enough Father, and too much Mother: he needed an essence of the absence to really release his stuff. Lew Welch did an amazing thing: he really cut loose with death.

Jack and Neal went within a year of each other at the end of the sixties: Jack was angry at the country; he was mad at Abbie Hoffman and Jerry Rubin for not getting the gist of his shy love, but making a slick vaudeville of the politics of America (the greasepaint and the guns almost indistinguishable, like when Andy Warhol got shot and created headlines, or later, people would mutilate themselves as an art form)—Jack was from a much simpler home and time and spirit and essence: he held his heart to be sacred, and looked into American television during his last years in Lowell in search of older virtues, and came away with a fondness for William Buckley, Jr. He was in a worse rebel hell at the end of his life than his beginnings could have hinted: he was an alcoholic sophisticate redneck in the middle of the melting clock of the sixties. When he moved his mother down to Florida, he was all but forgotten. He'd just gotten a phone installed on his kitchen wall in his new home—with his wife, Stella—when he had a massive hemorrhage which killed him, and his face made the network news—the face of 1957, with the open lumberjack shirt and a crucifix, the famous face of the Beat Generation, almost forgotten.

Neal was gone a year before, gone by the railroad tracks in the middle of Mexico, the juggling had gotten riddled with too many chemical mixes, too many un-stoppable karmic yawps and gals and flaks and impasses, toughs and grumble-ups, so that he, Neal, was like a living museum (that young guys would hurry to talk to) of the amazing circuits of the mind unwedded to anything beyond, say, a little speed, a little weed—and Neal's final number: throwing a hammer up into the air, so it somersaulted dozens of times up, dozens of times down—and he caught it, and threw it back up again, while he elaborated, or sometimes would just be silent, during the demonstration.

By now his face was a mask of itself, would not admit or betray any more than its own intent, unrelated, energy. He had not had a family at all: he had pursued his life on pure nerve, and delivered himself to his generation, and been given instruments and chemicals to make his movie move, and taken comfort in marijuana, which makes the mind up in its own way, and speed which makes it up another way, and Jack who loved him, and Carolyn who loved him, and being a Brakeman, and re-capping tires, and then getting together with Ken Kesey's Merry Pranksters and spiking the punch for a new generation: acid-heads.

They found his naked body by the railroad tracks; his eyes were out of town; his pulse was out to lunch; his back and balls and wrists and hair and feet and toenails, the scars and moles he had known his own life by, all slack and heavy and gone and done, all used up: that flashing, dashing enterprise of absolute glad creases and speeches, mixes and dishes, food and thought complexes: Neal. Whew. His heart had given out under the final mysterious enveloped circumstance under the Mexican sun (like poor Joan Burroughs). Allen Ginsberg delivered Neal's ashes to Carolyn. Allen older, bearded, shambling through the massive earth-tremors and blow-outs of the years: on acid in Bixby Canyon praying for the President of the United States to guide him in office and through the disease of war in Vietnam. Allen surviving.

And Lew dying, then, with a kind of perfection and splendor that was in advance of the studies of the subject now in currency. After returning from Forks of Salmon in January of 1964, and living through the decade in a home in Marin City with Magda Cregg, the last woman of his life, the one he remained with longest, and working as a longshoreman's checker on the waterfront, and teaching a poetry workshop at San Francisco State Extension, and giving many readings, and becoming a kind of Bay Area celebrity—yet all the time drinking more and more, talking more and more brilliantly, not writing very much, but making all of it close to flawless: simple, direct, entertaining, deep, natural, fluent, like the spring water on Mount Tamalpais, where he sometimes hiked and observed the Turkey Buzzards, the vultures that eat the dead, saw them from below on the mountain, saw them from above on the mountain, and Lew a man, and the bird a bird: and Lew could see this was the creature he rode, the creature he was in the deepest recesses of himself: the crack shot, who liked to glide, and yet this bird had the ability to eat anything (instead of being a starving—from B vitamin deficiency—alcoholic, who had to remind himself to feed himself: very confused)—this bird would eat anything.

Including Lew himself. And in his final poem, "Song of the Turkey Buzzard," which is the masterpiece of his career as a poet, one of the great American poems, he writes about his death, and explains it:

Hear my Last Will and Testament:

Among my friends there shall always be
one with proper instructions
for my continuance.

Let no one grieve.
I shall have used it all up
used up every bit of it.
What an extravagance!
What a relief!

On a marked rock, following his orders,
place my meat.

All care must be taken not to
frighten the natives of this
barbarous land, who
will not let us die, even,
as we wish.

With proper ceremony disembowel what I
no longer need, that it might more
quickly rot and tempt

my new form

Lew was looking forward with apparent joy to re-entering the Food Chain from a new angle, perhaps the healing angle of the Turkey Buzzard itself, who made no finicky distinctions about food: who ate everything, as Lew didn't know how to eat. The Turkey Buzzard who would eat Lew. And Lew knew this to be a traditional form of burial among the Tibetans, the Zoroastrians, the Amer/Indians—feeding the body of the dead to vultures.

And the hopeless alcoholic that Lew was nevertheless managed to see the poem through. In January of 1971 he and Magda Cregg split, and that spring Lew moved onto land in the foothills of the Sierra Nevada where he intended to build his own cabin on land adjacent to Gary Snyder's.

But he couldn't stop drinking; he was shot, had used it all up. He'd gone on Antabuse, which made it impossible for him to drink for 48 hours, but then let himself get off it, had a few beers—in the privacy of his van where he lived, eating with the Snyders—and the alcohol penetrated all the crevices and deep shores of death and mayhem in his spirit and body which a few beers don't reach in any but the alcoholic (as if the alcohol knows the man's psyche and spirit, his whole terrain, and holds it in its own will), and then saw himself: cleanly, clearly, finished.

And Antabuse is known to be a severe depressant.

So Lew must have seen his poem coming up cleanly and clearly now. He wrote a note in a notebook, appointing Donald Allen his literary executor. He took his revolver and walked away into the mountains.

Gary Snyder found the empty beer cans in his van, couldn't find Lew, read the note, got together thirty-five or forty people from the community, and for five days they searched—people crawling on their hands and knees through the manzanita; others firing rifle signals off various peaks to keep in touch with each other. They couldn't find Lew, and they decided to stop. Finally, it seemed obscene to search for a man who was so obviously determined not to be found.

And so the poet Lew Welch, forty-four, disappeared. The

final lines of the Turkey Buzzard poem speak from the depths of his own final mystery with undisguised joy:

NOT THE BRONZE CASKET BUT THE BRAZEN WING
SOARING FOREVER ABOVE THEE O PERFECT
O SWEETEST WATER O GLORIOUS
WHEELING

BIRD